The Wonder of Polymer Clay

Bonnie McGough

To Lisa with my Best Wishes
Bonnie McGough

Gibson Publishing

First published in the UK by Gibson Publishing

The Wonder of Polymer Clay

Layout and design by Bonnie McGough

A CIP catalogue record for this title is available from the British Library.

ISBN 978-0-9567101-2-3

The Wonder of Polymer Clay

Ideas and projects to inspire and guide the novice and the more experienced user

Bonnie McGough
Pendants

The Wonder of Polymer Clay

A humble journey into the Polymer Clay World

Bonnie McGough

Images by Chris Prasetyo

Bonnie's Lizards

This book is for Rieka Hughes, the lovely welsh voice, my guide, mentor and friend.

This book is also for Philip, my very supportive husband and soulmate.

Contents

Introduction

When we were children, my sister and I would spend every summer in the Rhodopi mountains. Small and pale, we stood out among the strong and sun-tanned village kids who lived there. They called us "the little white ones". The adults would work all day in the mountains and, left to our own devices, we would wander through the forest to play. The air was thick with the fragrance of pine and wild geranium. The water in the rivers we swam in was clear and clean enough to drink. When we got hungry, we would feast on the strawberries, blueberries and hazelnuts that grew wild in the forest. I am sure there were wild animals around — bears, wolves, boars — but I can't remember ever being afraid. In my memory of those summers, it was always sunny and pleasant, and I felt safe.

One day, a village kid took us to a spot where she said the earth was good. It must have been pure kaolin there. We would sit in Grandma's backyard making little houses. I still remember the tiny tables and chairs propped with sticks, the mini plates and bowls. The Rhodopi mountains were rich in quartz and you could peel it off in layers thin enough to see through. I would collect the tiny pieces and put them on to my creations. That was the first time I fell in love with clay.

Decades later, living in England, I owned a small boutique selling arts and crafts. On a whim I decided to stock Fimo - Polymer clay. When I opened up a block of clay and pressed it between my fingers, I was not prepared for the flood of memories of my childhood in the mountains.

I have been using the clay ever since, enjoying the play, the learning and later the teaching. It has been a wonderful journey into this exciting world of polymer clay. In my teaching years I have met many creative, artistic people, who have inspired me with their enthusiasm and willingness to learn.

My hope in writing this book is to share what I have learned over all those years. I want to guide you in enjoying a wonderful hobby and share my experiences with you. So, for all of you: this book is my world and I welcome you in.

Here I will show you the work with polymer clay as it is, not dolled up and made to look so perfect, that you are afraid to start. There will be blemishes and mistakes and fingerprints and "oooops... I can do better next time". I will tell you how to avoid some mistakes, but most of all I will guide you along the way to a most enjoyable hobby. So, come in and join me.

May this book inspire you to be playful, mischievous and curious, and to be touched by the same sense of wonder I knew when I was a child.

What is Polymer clay?

Polymer clay is a manmade modelling material and is a composite of polyvinyl chloride (PVC), plasticisers, pigments and fillers. It is called Polymer clay because of its resemblance of the texture and touch of natural earth clay.

In a raw state, Polymer clay is fairly soft and pliable, and will only harden when "cured", which means baked at a low temperature. Once baked, the clay can be sanded, drilled and is very hard to the touch.

There are many different makes of Polymer clay on the market. I have tried all of them but the ones I prefer to use are Fimo, followed by Cernit. There is a newish one on the market, called Cato clay, but I have found it rather difficult to condition. I choose to work with Fimo because it is so easy to condition, easy to use, comes in a wonderful range of colours and has simple baking instructions. In fact, you can bake your work of art several times, as long as you do not exceed the required oven temperature.

There are a few ranges of Fimo: the Fimo Classic range is mostly used for sculpting, modelling and Millefiori while the Fimo Soft is the most popular range for beginners and those using it as a general hobby.

The two ranges can be mixed very well. For sculpting and Millefiori I use three parts of Fimo Classic to one part of Fimo Soft. For all other uses, I have a mixture of half and half. When working normally with Polymer clay, there is no need to wear latex or non latex gloves, but if you are going to be a heavy user, I recommend the use of very fine latex gloves.

Storing and caring for your clay

Polymer clay will stay soft and pliable unti baked. The best way to store unopened blocks is at room temperature in a place away from heat and direct sunlight. The opened blocks are best stored in a heavy plastic boxes. There is no need for the boxes to be airtight, as long as they have good fitting lids. It is best to use heavy plastic boxes because the clay reacts chemically with the transparent light plastic variety, so do take care to choose the correct box.

Baking Instructions

Different makes of Polymer clay do not have the same baking times and temperatures. So it is important to follow the manufacturers instructions. For Fimo, the baking temperature is 110 degrees C for a minimum of 30 minutes. As it is possible to bake Fimo creations more than once, it is important to keep the temperature strictly at 110 degrees C. Once I did not like the head of a cat I had sculpted, so I decapitated the poor thing. Then I made a new head, attached it to the headless body and even gave it a hat and a scarf. In the oven it went and when it came out , it was pur....fect !

So before you bake any of your creations, check your oven. The best way to have the correct oven temperature is to invest in an oven thermometer. Oven thermometers are not expensive and I am still surprised that whenever I mention them in my workshops, people seem to shy away from the idea of buying one. Also, for fan-assisted ovens, it is important to follow the manufacturers' instructions and reduce the temperature accordingly.

For baking beads, the temperature is still 110 degrees C, but I bake them for one hour. This makes the beads much stronger. Bake on a dedicated baking tray, and use the tray strictly only for baking polymer clay. It is important not to mix the clay baking trays with ones you use for baking food.

Tools

The best surface to work on is a smooth floor or bathroom tile. A glass surface is also good to work on, but is more expensive and requires more care.

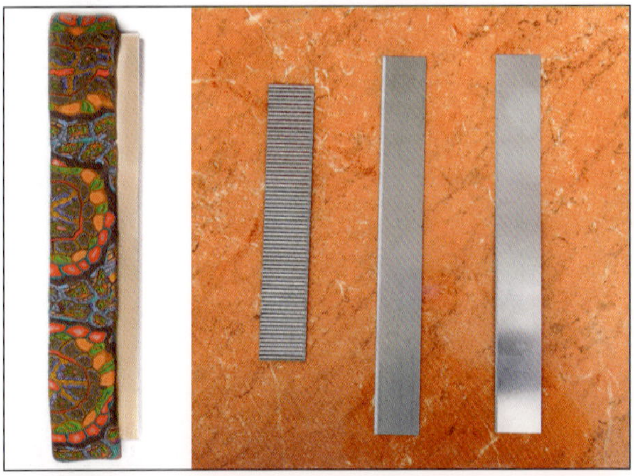

For cutting and shaping the clay, you will need a good craft knife. For millefiori and circular cutting it is best to have tissue blades. The blades are available in rigid or flexible form and are most useful for making canes. For the tissue blade on the left I made a scabbard to protect the blade. I had a slightly damaged cane left from a project, but it still looked good, so instead of discarding it, I found a use for it.

To roll out the clay, any roller made of glass, steel or acrylic will perform very well. The polymer clay will stick to rollers made of wood, and the normal rolling pins are totally unsuitable. So leave those to the cooking drawers.

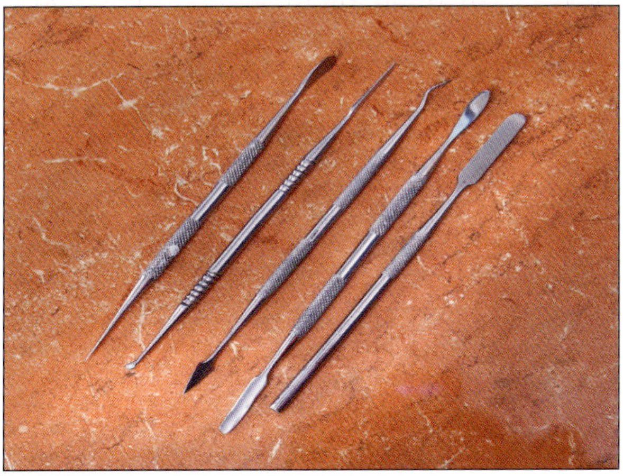

One of my favourite tools is the wax carving sculpting dental tools - the most versatile and useful tool in sculpting and general hobby work. With those tools I have sculpted the very large cats and dogs.

Pasta machine

Pasta machines can be used for conditioning the clay, blending colours, and rolling out very thin layers of clay. For me it is one of the basic tools, a must-have for cane making.

Extruder

There are a few 'extruders' or hair tools on the market. The best ones for me are the Makin extruder and the Tritools icing gun, shown in the picture on the left.

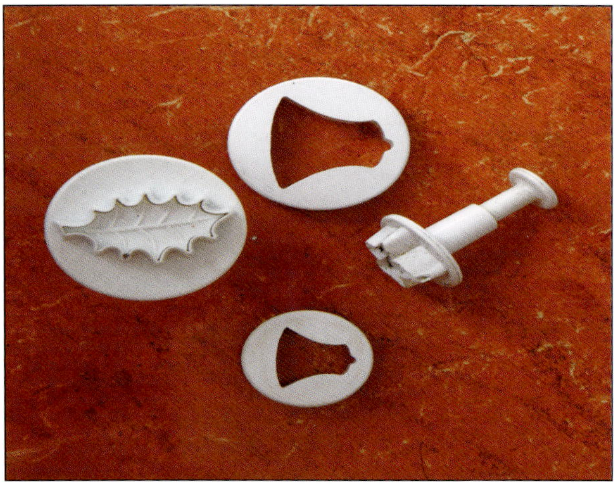

Cutters are time saving tools.
They can double also as texture tools and are such fun to collect,

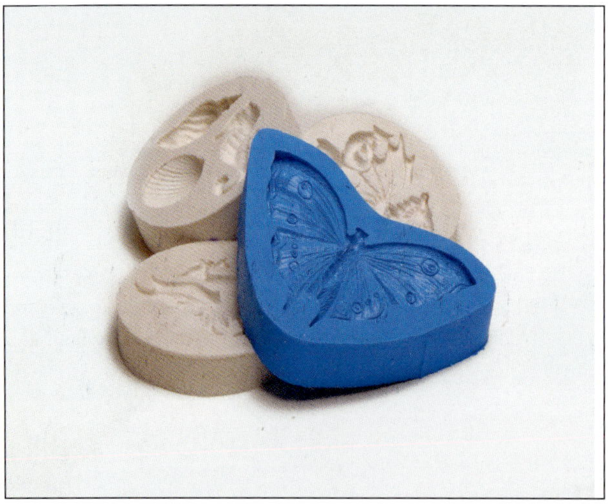

Silicone moulds

Silicone moulds are most suitable for use with polymer clay and the easiest to use. There is no need to dust with talcum powder when in use and they are flexible when removing the clay.

Cocktail sticks

Cocktail sticks are used to position small pieces of clay and beads and for making dots on the clay. It is surprising how useful this inexpensive tool is. On one of my visits to New York, in a tiny shop in Queens, I found this little jar full of cocktail sticks. I decorated it with leftover canes and it has been constantly admired at my workshops and demonstrations. It has travelled with me since all over Britain, and I am taking it to Ireland soon. So this will soon be my globetrotting little jar.

The bead rollers

These are available in many different shapes and sizes, but the most useful is the small Magic roller. It comes with a measuring device. I made some small colourful sticks with leftover Fimo canes and I use them to push the clay out. I call them my 'Dodaas'. This very useful tool is fun to use and fun to make.

Storage jars

Decorated lids on tiny jam jars, pill and trinket boxes. In the tall one with the friendly bug I keep my metallic gold powder. The bug keeps my gold safe. The honey bee looks after my petite glass beads. The ladybirds on the trinket box take care of the seed beads. The beads are used for the eyes on the small animals, the angels and the ladies.

Tools

Some of my tools I have enhanced by covering their handles. Other tools I made by adapting quill pen nibs and manipulating pieces of tin metal strips.

Texture tools

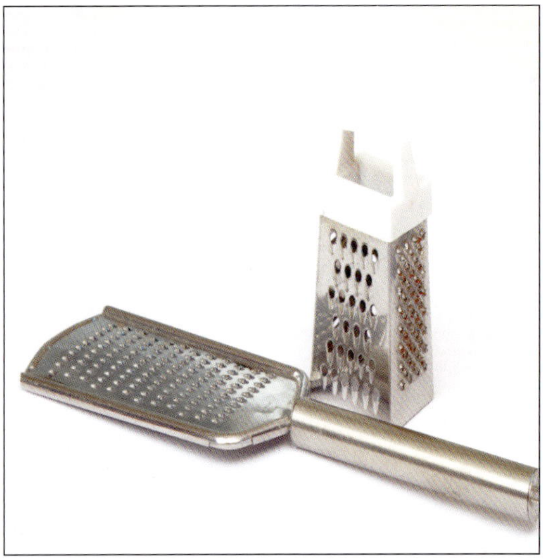

Graters are used for some techniques on unbaked and also baked clay.

Electric drill

I "borrowed" my husband's drill and this was the last time he could call it his. Once you have a tiny hole in the bead to guide your drill, enlarging the bead hole is very easy.

Wet and dry

Once clay is baked, it can be sanded, polished, cut. It is a very user friendly artistic medium.

Conditioning the clay

This is a very quick way to condition the clay with the help of a pasta machine. Take the amount you want to use and slice the thinnest slices you can with the tissue blade. I must confess, I have developed a bad habit of cutting the clay towards my fingers, and although I have not cut myself yet, please start better than me: cut away from your fingers!

With a tissue blade cut very thin slices of clay. Place slightly overlapping slices on the tile.

Roll the clay out with acrylic roller four to five times.

Put the rolled out clay through the pasta machine on the thickest setting.

Fold clay and put through the pasta machine again, starting with the folded side nearest to the rollers. This is very important, as rolling away from the fold prevents air pockets forming in the clay.

Repeat the process until the clay is soft and pliable.

The sample on the left shows frayed edges. This indicates that the clay has not been conditioned yet. When the clay is conditioned the frayed edges disappear.

Conditioning the clay without a pasta machine

Slice the required amount of clay, and if it is too large, cut it into smaller parts. Take the clay and roll it between the palms of your hands forming a ball. Roll the ball into a thick cylinder and then a ball again. Repeat until the clay becomes soft and pliable.

When you have more than one colour to condition, always start with the lightest colour. Always clean your hands before you start conditioning the clay. Also, when working with different colours always clean your hands between handling the colours.

The best wipes to use are wet hand wipes with added aloe or shea butter. I use Huggies baby wipes with shea butter. They not only clean my hands well, but also moisturise them. The wipes are very good for cleaning your tools and also the pasta machine. And one more useful tip: the wipes clean off any Fimo stuck on carpets.

Skinner blend

The Skinner blend is the nicest way of blending two or more colours. Invented by Judith Skinner, it has greatly benefited the polymer clay world. It is difficult to imagine polymer clay colour blending without the Skinner blend. So here is the way to do a Skinner blend: enjoy the results of this seamless grading of the colours method.

Materials:

1/2 block white clay
1/2 block purple clay

Condition clay starting with the white clay. Roll out and cut two equal triangles, equal in size, equal in thickness. Position the triangles to form a rectangle and run through the pasta machine on the thickest setting.

Fold the rectangle as shown on the picture and roll through the pasta machine starting with the fold. This prevents air pockets being trapped in the clay. Repeat the roll and fold the rectangle always in the same direction, away from the fold.

When you achieve smooth colour transition, turn rectangle 90 degrees and pass through the pasta machine starting with the lighter colour.

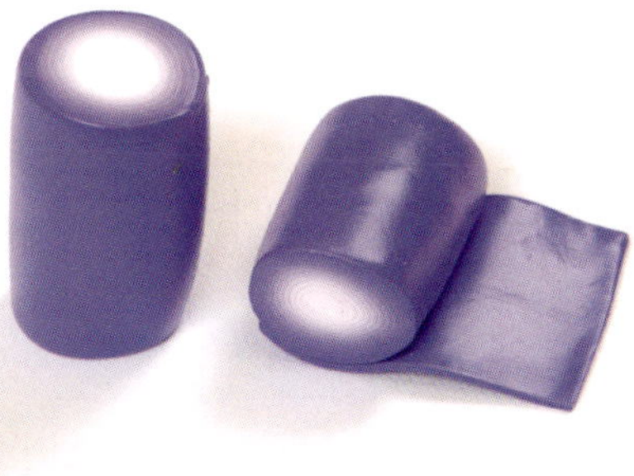

Colour blending without a pasta machine

Materials:

1/2 block light green
1/2 block dark green

Condition clay and form two cubes. Mark the top of the cubes as on the pictures above, then cut vertically with a tissue blade.

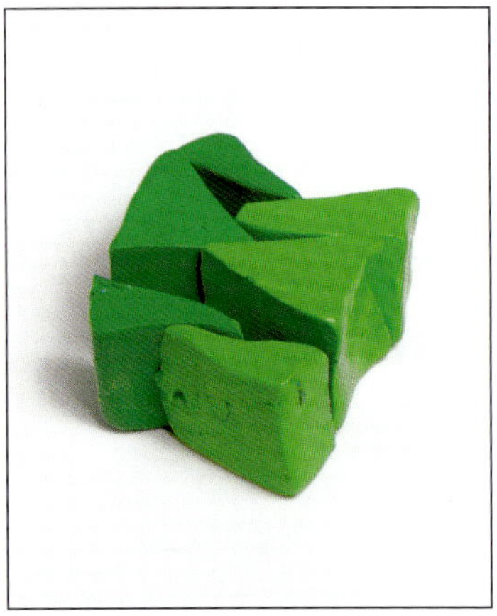

Position the colour as above and make a larger cube. Flatten cube slightly and then roll further with the acrylic roller. Cut across and stack. Flatten with the acrylic roller and cut again.

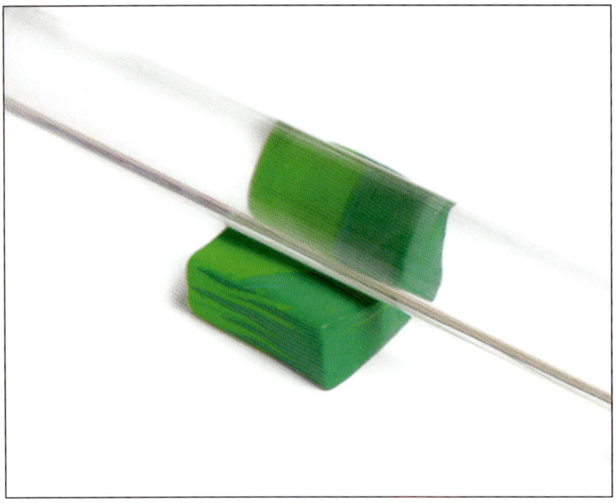

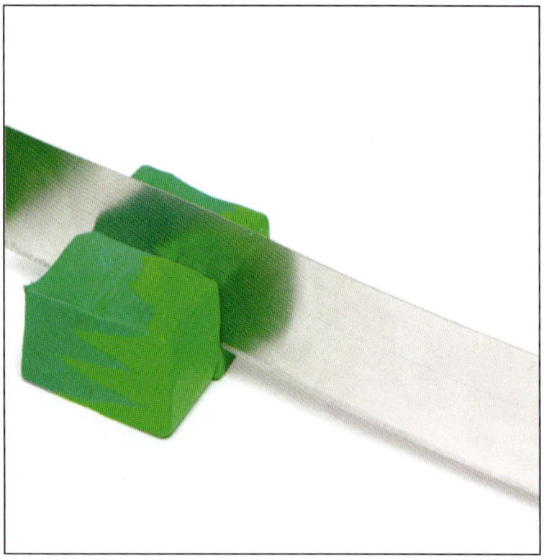

Repeat the cut and stack, then roll out again.

Repeat this step until you achieve a smooth colour blend.
The more times you repeat the step, the better the blend will be.

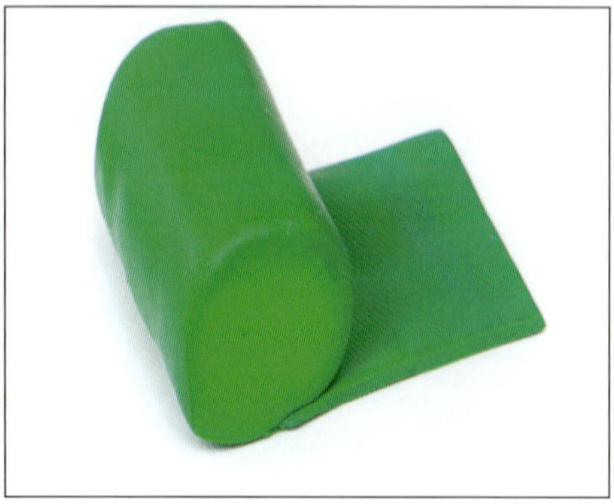

Once the colour blend is achieved, flatten the cube with the roller from the lighter coloured end toward the dark coloured end. Roll out a few times, until you achieve a long strip, then roll into a cylinder.

Millefiori

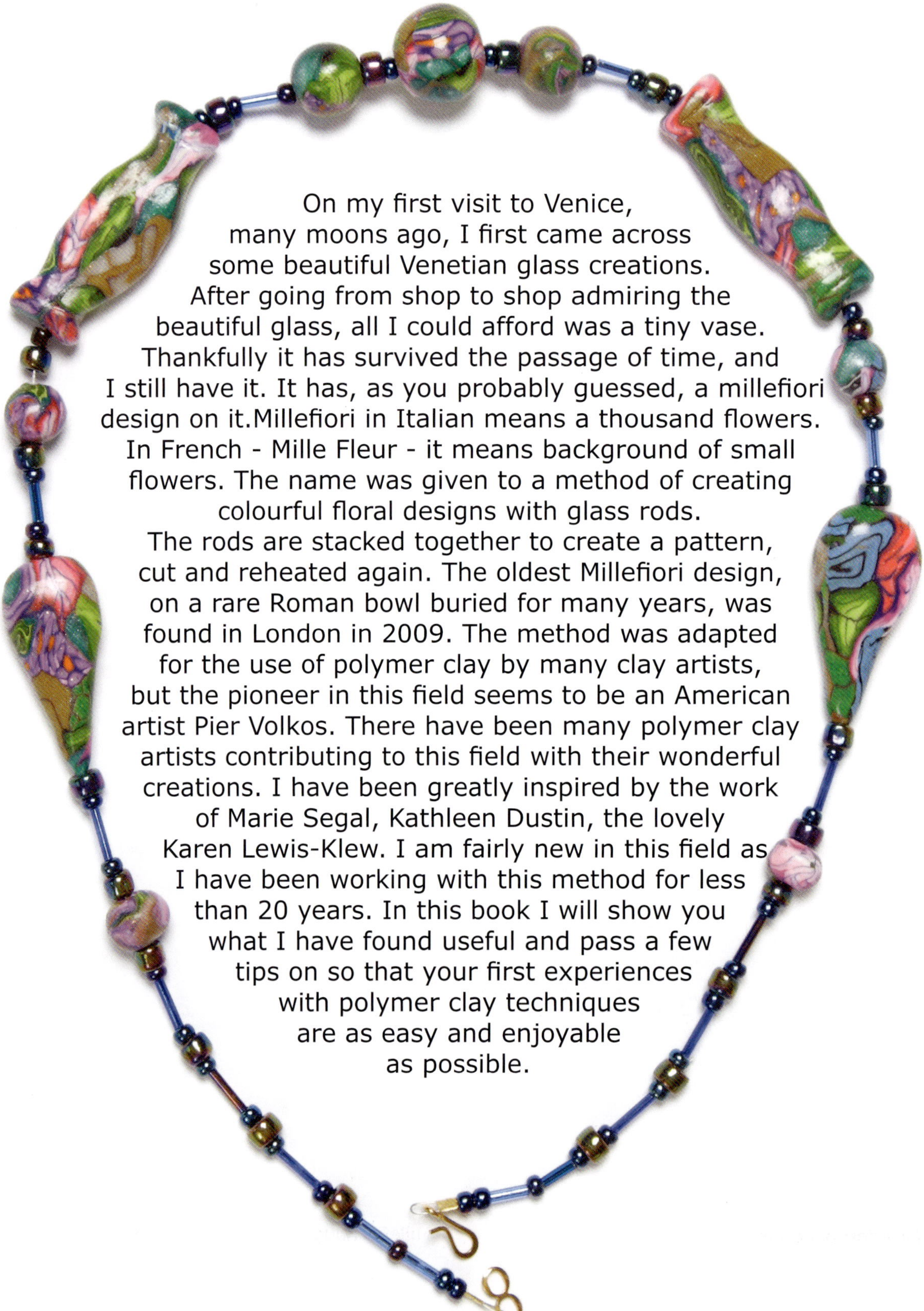

On my first visit to Venice, many moons ago, I first came across some beautiful Venetian glass creations. After going from shop to shop admiring the beautiful glass, all I could afford was a tiny vase. Thankfully it has survived the passage of time, and I still have it. It has, as you probably guessed, a millefiori design on it.Millefiori in Italian means a thousand flowers. In French - Mille Fleur - it means background of small flowers. The name was given to a method of creating colourful floral designs with glass rods. The rods are stacked together to create a pattern, cut and reheated again. The oldest Millefiori design, on a rare Roman bowl buried for many years, was found in London in 2009. The method was adapted for the use of polymer clay by many clay artists, but the pioneer in this field seems to be an American artist Pier Volkos. There have been many polymer clay artists contributing to this field with their wonderful creations. I have been greatly inspired by the work of Marie Segal, Kathleen Dustin, the lovely Karen Lewis-Klew. I am fairly new in this field as I have been working with this method for less than 20 years. In this book I will show you what I have found useful and pass a few tips on so that your first experiences with polymer clay techniques are as easy and enjoyable as possible.

Janice Cooper
Millefiori necklace and bracelet

Bonnie McGough
Millefiori pendant

Bonnie McGough
Millefiori bug

Jana Roberts Benzon exquisite cane work
Arabesque Collage Pendant

Jana Roberts Benzon
Stonegarden

Klew - Karen Lewis
Some truly wonderful cane work
www.klewexpressions.com

Simple cane

Materials:

1/3 block blue
1/8 block black

Condition blue clay and make into a cylinder. Make the cylinder approximately 1 1/2 inch high to 1 inch wide.

Condition black clay and roll out on the thinnest setting on your pasta machine.

Position the cylinder, laying it on its side, on the black sheet of clay. Trim excess black clay.

Roll the cylinder until it is evenly covered with black clay, and again trim any excess of black clay.

This is the basic simple cane. Now you are ready to do all sorts of manipulations and create beautiful millefiori.

Important tip: when making canes it is best to leave the canes to REST. This allows the cane to cool and harden so that the shape of the cane will not distort, particularly when making flowers or stacking and more complex canes. It is best to leave the canes as long as two days or four hours in the fridge.

Flower cane

Materials:

1/2 block blue clay
1/2 block white clay
1/8 black clay
1/16 yellow or red clay

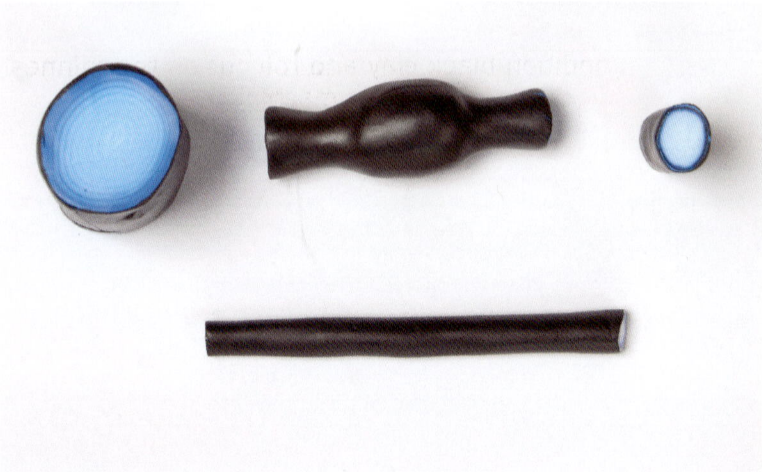

Make a simple cane with one colour or a Skinner blend cane with the white and the blue clay.

Reduce the cane by squeezing it at both ends to the width you wish your petals to be. Roll out by the palm of your hands. This way you will have an even long rod.

Mark the rod using a ruler, and cut into sections to make five or six petals. I have chosen a flower with five petals. After you have cut your petals, condition the yellow clay.

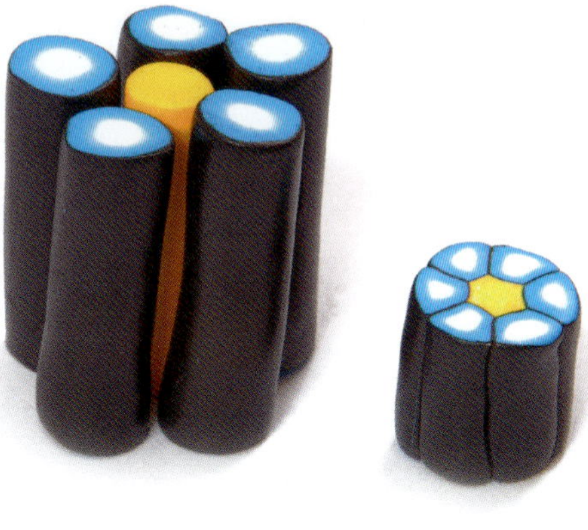

Make the yellow cylinder slightly thinner than the petal canes. Trim the yellow cylinder to the same length as the petal canes. Assemble the flower as displayed on the picture.

Leaf cane

Materials:
1/2 block light green
1/2 block dark green
1/8 block black

Make a Skinner blend and form a cylinder. Condition and roll out black clay on the thinnest setting on the pasta machine.

Cut vertically into three equal sections. Take care to keep the tissue blade straight.

Position the first slice on the black clay. Trim around and replace in the original position. Take the third slice and repeat, placing it on the black as with the previous slice.

Put the third slice back in its original position. This picture is of the cane after the black clay has been added and turned 45 degrees ready to be sliced vertically in the centre .

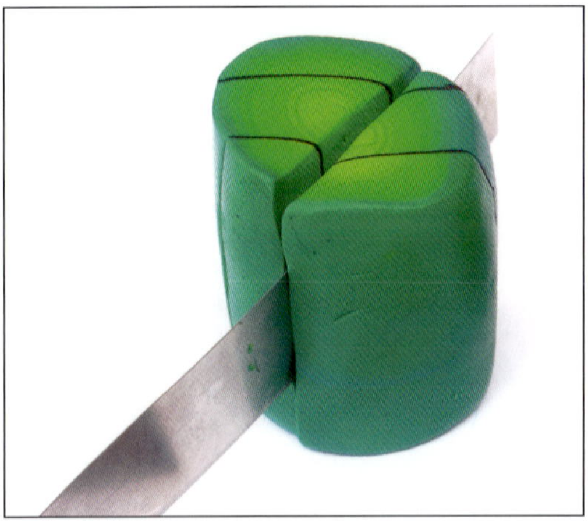

Turn the cane about 45 degrees and cut vertically straight down the centre. Remember to hold the blade very straight, as it is very easy to deviate and cut unevenly.

Place a thin layer of black clay in the centre and trim.

Take the left section and turn it upside down.

Join the two sections together. Now you have a leaf with the veins facing the correct way.

On this picture I have added a small wedge at the base of the leaf and also wrapped extra thin layers of contrasting colour. This made the leaf slightly different. Use your imagination and add extra colours and see the wonderful results.

Bonnie McGough
The seahorse

Have you heard that in the Birmingham Water World, they are separating the male seahorses from the females....for their own protection? The male seahorses needed protection from the constant romantic attention of the females. I am not sure what I made here - a male or female. It could be a male refugee!

Bonnie McGough
Japanese kokeshi doll

Leaf variation from the peacock feather

This leaf is a variation of the peacock's feather. So look at the peacock's feather page and for the beginning of the cane follow the instructions until this step.

Condition about 1/16 of black clay and roll it out very thin.

Position the centre of the cane on the black clay, and trim the excess black clay off.

Join the two halves of the cane as on the picture. The leaf is now ready for use, but as it is still soft, leave the cane to REST. This makes the slicing of the cane much easier and prevents any distortion.

Complex canes

This is where the millefiori becomes most exciting. To create complex canes you can use the basic plane cane and mix with with other canes or wrap the basic canes with extra colours. It is so much easier to make the canes with polymer clay than glass.

Complex canes

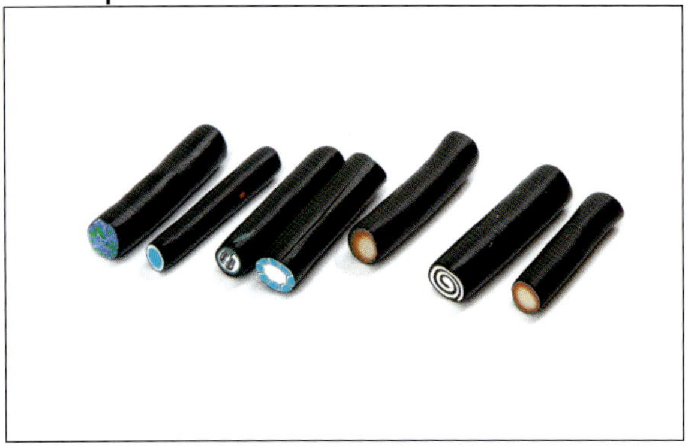

Decide on the colours that you want to use and make a few simple canes. In the next couple of pages I will show you how to add to canes or make different ones.

This is a simple jelly roll cane.

Condition two colours of your choice and roll out on the thick set on your pasta machine. Whichever colours you choose, make sure you use equal quantities of clay. Place the first colour on top of the second colour.

At one end trim the lighter colour diagonally, leaving the bottom colour a couple of millimetres longer. Roll out gently with the roller to eliminate any air pockets forming between the sheets of clay.
Starting from one end roll the two sheets together to form the jelly roll.

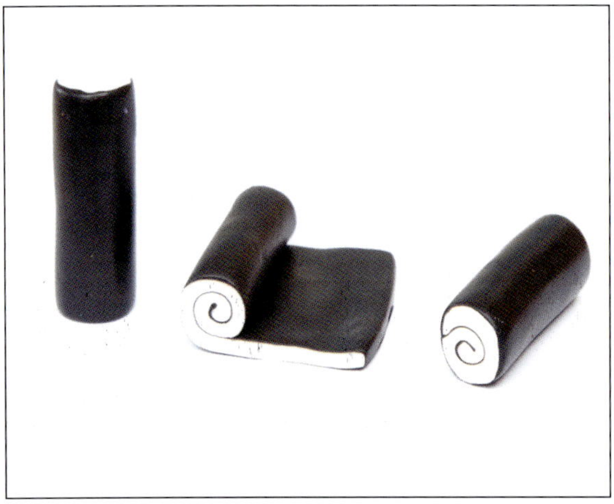

There is a variation to the jelly roll cane. Make a cane and flatten slightly by hand and then roll out more with an acrylic roller. Roll out about 2 to 3 times its diameter. Roll as the jelly roll.

This makes the same design as the jelly roll but with finer lines inside.

Complex canes

This cane is made with leftover clay and scrap clay. Make whatever colours you have left and in any quantity into different width canes, but trim to equal length. Stack them together and wrap round with any contrast colour you like.

I have used black here, but the cane will look good with any dark colour. I had a small blue cane to spare and it was just long enough to make the centre of my complex cane.

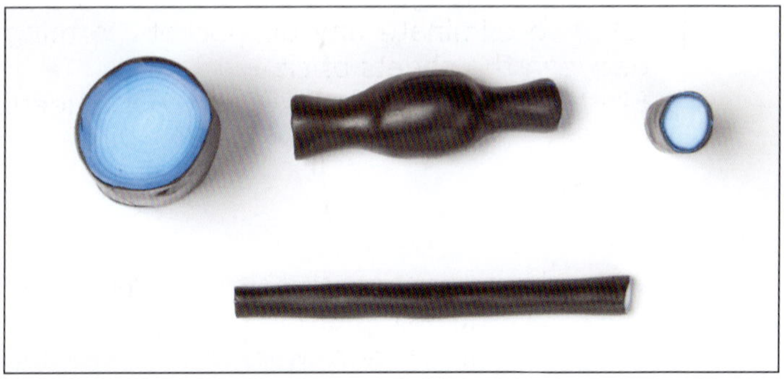

Reduce the multicoloured cane into very slim long rod and cut enough rods to wrap the centre cane with. Cut all rods to the same length as the centre cane.

For the outside, make a Skinner blend cane, it does not have to be the same colour blue as the inside. Until now I have not specified exact amounts of materials needed at the start of this project because this is a way to experiment yourself with how much clay you will need.

So if your cane so far is about one inch in diameter, you will have to do the outer blue cane about 1 1/2 inches in diameter. For this you will need 1/2 block white clay and 1/2 block blue clay and 1/8 of black clay to wrap round it.

Make the last blue Skinner blend cane. Reduce and cut the same way as on the previous round.

Stack the blue rods around the multicoloured cane. When making any cane it is good to remember to let the cane REST. The longer you leave any cane to rest, the better result you will have.

The cane can be left for 2 hours in the fridge, or even longer. Also some artists leave their canes for couple of days. So, if you want perfection, find some patience and let your canes REST.

Mishaps and mistakes

I have tried throughout the book to show you the real way the work is done, and not a cleaned upn version. The hands you see in the book are my own very old hands. The blemishes and little faults on the canes and the finger prints are also all mine.

I wanted to show you how it really looks when you first start, and to stop you from worrying if your initial creation is not absolutely perfect. It won't be because perfection comes with practice. But in this field practice is fun.

To clean blemishes on the unbaked clay gently wipe with baby wipes. I love the ones with added shea butter. Baby wipes also remove fingerprints from unbaked clay.

A great tip for picking up tiny bits of clay from unbaked clay is to use Blu Tack. It removes them without marking the clay. Finally if you have blemishes or a dirty mark you want to remove after baking, use the fine wet and dry sand paper.

Kaleidoscope canes

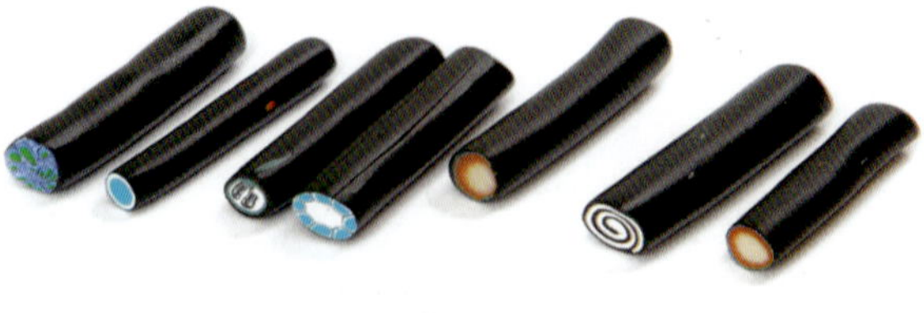

This is a kaleidoscope cane, one of the basic complex canes. It is just a way of stacking different canes, shaping the stacked canes into a triangular cane and then making square or hexagonal canes with the triangles.

Who invented it first? Maybe the one who found out that blue and yellow together make green!

If you play with the canes and experiment, sooner or later you will make one of those. So use your imagination and experiment, play, enjoy.

In the jewellery section you will be able to see further use of these easy and very versatile canes to make. I love making these canes as I always have so many small "leftover" canes, and throwing any canes together seem to work for me every time.

Bonnie McGough
The peacock

Peacock feather

Materials:
1/4 of a block of five different shades of green
1/8 block black
1/16 light green

Condition colours, starting with the lightest colour. Place them together to form a cube.

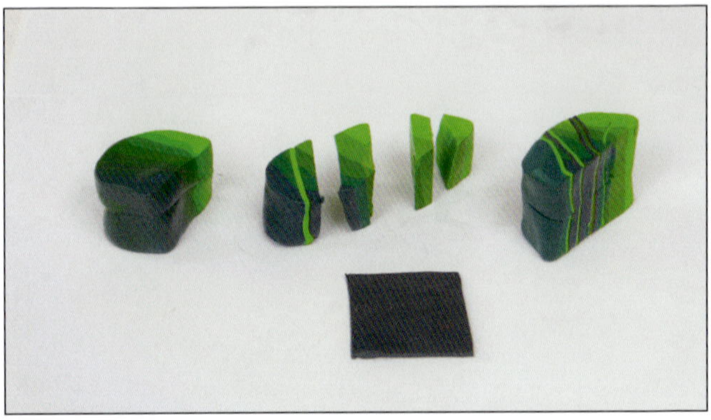

Make the cube into a crescent shape.

Make five diagonal cuts.
Condition and roll out light green clay.

Roll the light green clay not too thin. Place inside the cuts. Then roll out the conditioned black clay and put next to the light green clay. Join the crescent together.

Turn the crescent on its flat side and cut into two. Turn the two sections toward each other.

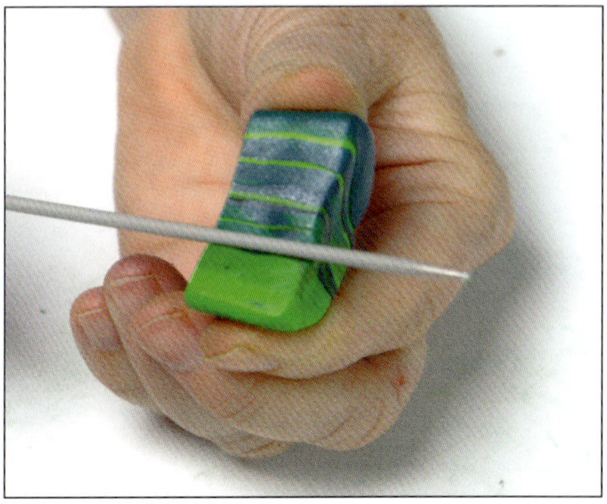

With a knitting needle make indentations on both sections.

Materials for the eye in the feather:

1/8 block pink clay
1/8 block blue clay
1/8 block gold clay
1/8 block black clay

Wrap a pink cylinder with a thin layer of black clay. Roll out the blue quite thick so that it just covers the pink, but leave a gap. Then roll out the gold and wrap again with a thin layer of black.

Add the thickly rolled out gold and roll out the cylinder to the desired length. Put the eye cane into the indents made with the knitting needle. Join the two sections. The feather cane is ready. Let it REST.

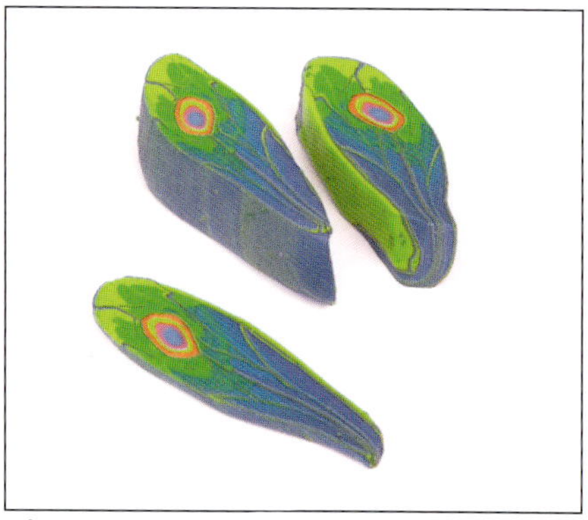

This is your ready peacock's feather cane.

Peacock feather 2

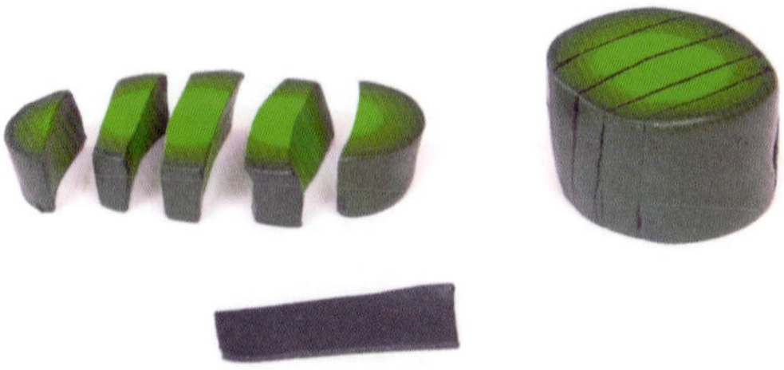

Materials:
1/1/4 light green
1/4 dark green
1/8 black
1/8 pink
1/8 blue

Make a Skinner blend cylinder. Cut four vertical cuts with a tissue blade. As for the leaf cane place thin black sheets of clay between the cuts.

Join the sections together. Wrap cylinder with a thin layer of black clay.

Flatten cane slightly, then roll with the acrylic roller twice the canes diameter. Make the eye by wrapping the pink clay around the blue.

Place eye cane at one end and roll as shown on the picture.
Roll the eye cane enough to just cover the eye cane without leaving a gap.
Your second feather cane is ready.

Bonnie McGough
Pendants

Mokume Gane

Mokume Gane is an old Japanese method for creating patterns on steel. When making swords, in order to strengthen the steel, thin layers were manipulated and fused together. This created wood grain-like patterns on the steel. So Mokume Gane means wood - eye-metal in Japanese. The technique has been adapted for use with polymer clay.

Layers of polymer clay are stacked together with many additives in between. The additives could be Mica powders, leaf metal, metallic powders,
liquid clay, acrylic or oil paint.

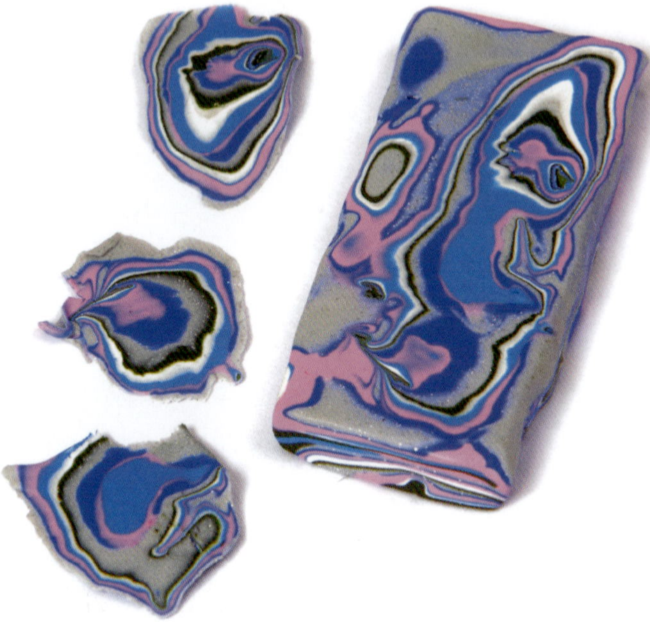

In some of my Mokume Gane efforts I have used black and green sparkling embossing powders. This techniques renders itself to lots of different interpretations with the most pleasing results.

Materials:
1/4 block translucent
1/4 black
1/4 purple
1/4 blue
1/4 silver
Pinch of black sparkle
Leaf metal - silver or gold
embossing powder

Condition clay, starting with the lighter colours. Roll out clay in same size rectangles. Alternate layers of any colour with leaf metal.

At this point as extra you can add a small amount of black sparkling embossing powder on the black layer.

When all layers are in place, roll the stack of clay to double size and cut into two. Place the second part on top of the first one.

Turn stack upside down and make very deep impressions on the clay. Use any tools, the back of a pencil or any texture tool for example. Push some translucent clay into the holes. Compress the rectangle inwards to create a smaller stack.

Before turning the stack back, with your fingers push the clay to form slightly raised points in the clay. Turn the stack up and with a tissue blade start cutting the clay horizontally.

Barbara McGuire
Bracelet

Barbara McGuire
Geisha transfers

The Honey Bee

Materials:

1/16 block yellow
1/4 block black
1/16 block translucent
1/16 block white
1/16 block white glitter

Condition all colours, starting with the lighter colours.

The body, head and legs.

Using all of the yellow clay roll out in a small rectangle. Do the same with black, using as much black as yellow clay. Place yellow clay onto the black. Cut the stack into two and stack again. You can leave it here, or add an extra black layer.

Form the body with the yellow/black stripe.

To make the head, make a small black ball. Also if you wish to add more detail, make the black ball and add a small yellow stripe at the base of the head. The legs are made of two small short strips of black clay.

Condition white clay and make a cylinder. Mix white glitter and translucent clays. Divide into two and make two cylinders.

So now you have two smaller cylinders made out of the mixture and a larger one in white. Make a cane, by placing the two smaller cylinders on the side of the larger white one.

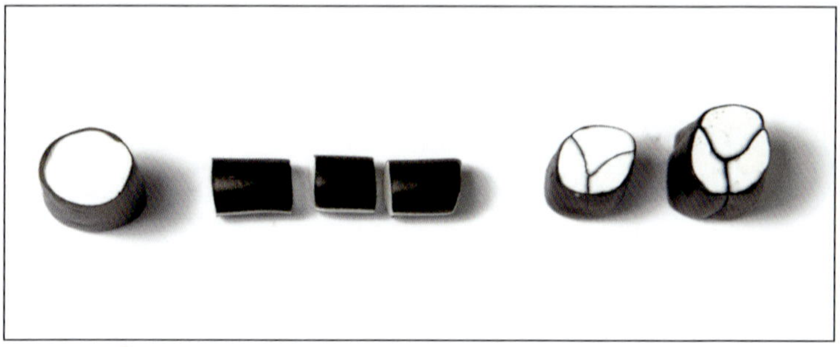

Press the three cylinders together to form one larger cylinder. Wrap the cylinder with very thin layer of black clay. Reduce cane and cut into three lengths.

Flatten the three canes very slightly and assemble to form the wing.

Assemble the honey bee.

As I use Fimo polymer clay, the baking instructions throughout this book apply only to Fimo polymer clay.

Bonnie McGough
Grandma's Cow

My Grandma's bad tempered cow

No amount of tempting with juicy grass could soften my Grandma's hard-hearted cow towards me.
In the farm they had hundreds of sheep, lots and lots of horses and goats and some more cows, but this one was my Grandma' s special cow. She only loved Grandma and nobody else, and that included me. Being a 'townie' I so much wanted to be friends with the cow, but she dismissed all my efforts of friendship. I suppose she did not have much time for a tiny little pest like me.
So here is an interpretation of a cow I have seen somewhere, a friendly one! It was never intended for show, but I will let you have a peep.

Angela Smith
Little Cows

The ladybird

Materials:
1/16 black clay
1 /16 red clay

Condition clay. Make a red ball, the size of a pea. Cut into two. Make a second ball half the size of a pea and shape into a tear drop.

The head can be the size of a small lentil or half a pea. There is a variable tolerance in the sizing of the head. Ladybirds look just as nice with smaller or larger heads.

The antennae also could be much larger than a real life ladybird antennae. Assemble the ladybird and position two tiny white dots for the eyes.

Paint black dots in the eyes with permanent black marker.

Using baking instructions for Fimo polymer clay: bake the ladybird in preheated oven at 110 degrees C for 30 minutes.

Butterfly and dragonfly wing canes

Materials:

1/2block white clay
1/4 block pink clay
1/2 block lavender clay
1/4 block black clay
1/4 block purple

Make simple canes. I have a selection of canes here to stack and make the butterfly's wing. The dark pink and white cane and the eye canes are made by adding extra layers of different colour clay to a simple cane.

If you experiment with colours, the results will be better then expected.

When the canes are all stacked, press firmly together and form the complex cane, which will be your butterfly wing.

Shape the wing in a butterfly wing shape to your liking, ignore the top layer. This is the messy layer. Slice it off.

At this point you can wrap the cane with extra layers of thin contrast colour clay, and then the final black layer.

There are so many variations of colours you can use, so do not limit yourself. The materials I have suggested for this cane are only a guidance.

Here is a shaped butterfly wing cane.

I reduced the cane, cut it into two and when stacking the two canes together added two extra eye canes in the middle.

This cane will be very good to use on the bug too. For using it on the bug, just change the shape of the cane.

When I demonstrate, I am often asked by people for ideas, rather than for exact guidance about materials needed. They ask for something to look at, for some inspiration and for something to copy.

So this cane is for you. Good luck, and make it better than mine!

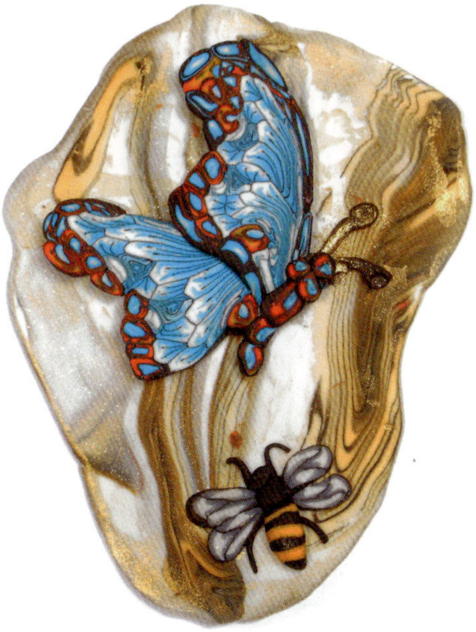

Bonnie McGough
The dragonfly

Materials:

The wings:

1/2 block white clay
1/2 block lavender clay
1/4 block black clay
1/4 block purple clay
1/4 block pink clay

The tail, head, antennae and legs:

1/16 block purple clay
1/16 block black clay
1/16 block pink clay

These materials are only a rough guidance. See the previous two pages for the butterfly wings. In the pictures below there are some more ideas for dragonfly wings.

The only difference from the butterfly wings is the shape of the wings.

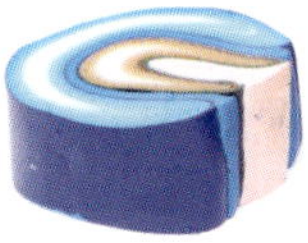

For the tail just wrap an extra colour or two to the simple cane.

Also roll out a simple cane and add a thin cylinder of a plain colour in and enclose by rolling it in the cane as on the picture above.

Make the tail by squeezing the tail cane to make a pointed tear drop shape.
Cut a thicker slice and flatten to make it bigger for the main body.

Take wing cane and cut four thick slices, about 4mm thickness. Assemble the wings as shown on the picture.

For the eyes cut two smaller slices and shape them round. Make one thick round slice for the head. Take a small amount of black clay and make the legs and the antennae and, as on the picture, add them to the body.

If you wish, at this point, you can add extra front and back legs to the dragonfly, This is your artistic expression. As I have used Fimo polymer clay to make the dragonfly, follow the these instructions: bake for 30 minutes at preheated oven at 110 degrees C.

Bonnie McGough
Thomas

These cats were my first large creations in Fimo. He is about 15 inches high and she is 12 inches high.

For making the frame body of the cats I used Wireform mesh and florist wire. Kitchen foil is normally used for medium sized animals.

The basic body was covered with scrap clay and then the top layers were made out of canes, stacked together in a very informal way.

Both cats were baked more than 4 times, from the first to the final stages of readiness.

Malinka is a very good companion for Thomas.

They live in happy harmony next to the frog, who is in love with the doll. But that is another story.

Bonnie McGough
Malinka

Bonnie McGough
The Welsh dragon - Cumru am byth

I have loved Wales ever since I first set foot in Milford Haven in the sixties, not long after I arrived in the UK.

I love the singing, the melodic accent, the people, and the rolling hills. After so many years I still remember the kindness and warm hospitality given to a very homesick me all those years ago. So Wales will always have a very special place in my heart.

Bonnie McGough
The Welsh dragon

The bug

Some of the creepy crawlies I spotted during my travels in Indonesia were such scary creatures that it is almost strange to see how much they have gone on to inspire me artistically.

In Ubud in the mountain region of Bali, I remember being mesmerised by a fight between a lizard and a most exotic big shimmering beetle.

Later in Jakarta, I tried to spot the elusive Tokay gecko in order to immortalise the little creature in polymer clay. Despite his famously deafening calls I was only rewarded with the briefest glimpse.

Therefore my creations have very little and possibly even no resemblance to the real thing, but I hope you will love them as much as I do.

For the bugs, again I use scrap clay canes, all sorts of leftover canes and never worry about the exact measure of the materials I start with. For you, I have made a great effort to work out some guidance about the easiest way to introduce you to making the canes for the bugs. I have used scrap clay, leftover canes and easy to make complex canes.

You do not need a great quantity of clay or big canes. Also the colours can be very easily substituted. Just use your imagination with whatever colour of clay you have available.

Materials:

Canes used for the bug on the right:
Pink flower cane
Brown leaf cane
Green leaf cane
Purple/white cane
Blue scrap clay cane
Pink plain cane
Rose cane on silver clay
Purple/black/pink scrap clay cane

This is a complex way to make the bug and it may not be suitable for the beginner, but don't let that stop you - have a go! I have simplified it as much as I can.

Materials for bug on the left:

1/3 block black clay
Pea size white clay
I inch ball of scrap clay
To make a bug in a size about 4 inches by 4 1/2 inches make the canes with the following:

Fast white cane:
1/8 block black clay
1/4 block white clay
1/4 block dark pink clay
1/4 block white clay
1/8 block black clay

Simple green cane
1/4 block green cane
1/8 block black clay

Fast pink cane:
1/4 block dark pink clay
1/4 block white clay
1/8 block black clay

Simple green cane:
1/4 block green cane
1/8 block black clay

These canes are for your guidance. Make the quick cane with any green clay and stack to make the complex cane. Stack in any order.

Add pink clay in the middle. Make the pink as a cylinder, so when you press the two canes together it will elongate in the middle.Then wrap the new cane with a thin pink strip, followed by a thin black strip of clay.

Make two canes, one quick white and one quick pink cane. For extra info, the pink cane was made with white and pink clay with the Skinner blend technique.

Here are a few more variations.

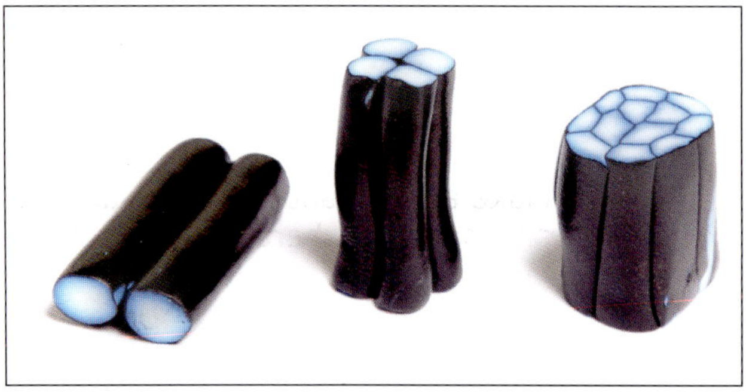

This is the easiest cane. A simple blue cane is stacked to for the complex blue cane - one more idea for you.

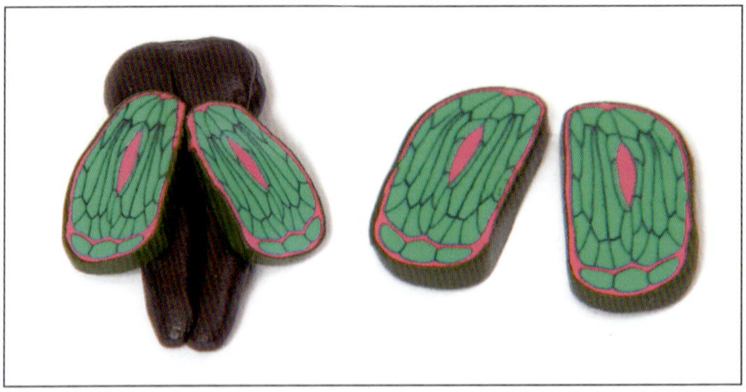

Make the body with a circle of scrap clay. The legs are made with black clay, rolled out into a slim rod and folded in two. Round the ends of the back legs and squeeze a little to make them very slightly tapered.

Cut two slices about 3mm thick for the first lot of under wings. Position as on the picture on the left.

Make two thinner legs and position by the first under wings.

Cut the pink cane like the first one. Cut two 3mm thick under wings and position on top of the first wings, allowing a lot of them to be seen.

The lighter cane for the third set of under wings is cut the same way as the previous wings. Position them as on the picture on the left.

This bug can have as many under wings as you wish as long as they are placed in a way to show as much as possible of the lower under wings.

Cut two more of the green cane, still 3mm thick. Lift the lighter wing and place the green ones as on the picture.

Make an oval shape from black clay and position where the head of the bug should be.

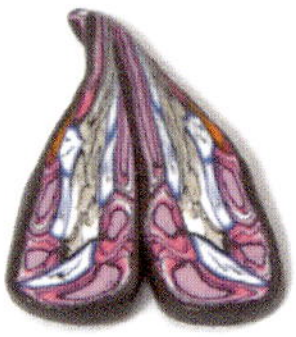

Cut two 3mm thick slices from the pink cane. Position side by side and squeeze at the top. Place in the centre, with the narrow end at the base of the head. Cut two 3mm thick green canes, place at the base of the head and leave standing straight.

Make a round shape out of the light coloured cane and press to make it an oval shape. Place it on the top of the base of the head. At this point if the head is on the small side add another ball of black clay pressing it firmly to the light cane oval. Make the eyes. Two white balls, two black balls. Position eyes in place.

As with most art projects, this is not a precise science. There are lots of ways you can alter any of the sizes or positions of the components. This is just a guide. Go for it....have a go and have fun. Change as much as you like and create a bug to remember.

Bonnie McGough
Red Millefiori fish

Bonnie McGough
Gold Millefiori fish

Ginka Puss

For as long as I can remember I have loved cats, and I have been surrounded by them throughout my life.

As children we played with them, allowed them to sneak into our beds and when we were discovered we faced the consequences.

In the passing years I have collected lots of paw prints in my heart.

There was Master Thomas Tucker, a gorgeous tabby and white cat, who went to the local infant school for his 'elevenses' every day. The school sent excellent reports back and when he died they held a remembrance service. Of course, handsome Thomas made the front page of the local paper.

Then there was Suki, a very smart, chocolate Burmese cat who lived to the grand old age of 19. I thought she could not be matched by any other cat for her good nature and her great character. Her expert door opening skills astonished all our guests. I grieved for her for years and still do.

But Ginka Puss was very special. She was a very mixed-up little rescue cat who spent a good few years hiding under the bed before becoming a warm and trusting companion.

The birds population in our garden was safe, as they were beyond her reach.The toads however became a focus of her attention with little succes on her part.

Her sudden departure from this world has been a great blow to me. I do miss my little Ginka cat.

The cat

Materials:
2 and 1/3 blocks black clay, 1 block white clay, 1/16 of green, yellow, red clay, Size of 1 block scrap clay
Cooking foil the size of a small pear,
Cocktail sticks

Make the body with the kitchen foil. Squeeze and press the foil with your hands to form a pear shaped body. At the top push a cocktail stick into the body allowing it to stick out about 1cm. Placing the cocktail stick in the body reinforces it, and makes positioning of the head very easy.

Now roll out scrap clay about 4mm thick and cover the body, by firmly pressing onto the foil.
Condition white clay, leave ready to use. Take 1/3 of the white clay and roll out to 4 mm thickness. Trim to a triangle shape and place on the body. Clean hands with wet wipes.

Take 1 block black clay, condition and roll out to a triangle. This will be the back and side of the body. Make a triangle and cut the top so it is not pointed. Measure the size of the trangle from the body and make the triangle approximately a size large enough to cover the back. Cover the back with the black clay triangle.

On the picture above, the black clay needs to be stretched slightly to fit. This is done very easily. It is better to do it this way, than to try to measure to make the exact triangle. It also helps to learn to work relying on your natural creative abilities.

Ginka Puss

Take 2/3 block black clay, condition and divide into two and make the back legs and the two paws for each leg. Attach the back legs to the body without the paws.
Take 2/3 of black clay and make the front paws and attach to the body, starting from the bottom. Cut any excess from the length of the front paws at the neck.

Add the two balls for the back paw pads to the back legs.
Take 1/3 of black clay, condition and make the cat's tail. Make the end of the tail nicely rounded and curl. Squash at the uncurled end about 1/2 cm with your hand. Place at the back, under the cat's body and guide to the front, curling it as shown on the picture.

Now you have a headless cat - poor thing! The fun of making the rest of the cat is just beginning.

Clean hands thoroughly. Try not to touch the white parts of the cat when moving it aside, as now is the time you can make so many dirty marks and leave your fingerprints.

Condition green clay and make a short thin cylinder.

Take black clay 1/2 the size of the green clay and roll out thick.Wrap round the green cylinder, leaving a gap uncovered. Clean hands.

Take white clay the size of the green and roll out thick, about 4mm approximately. Wrap round the black. Then roll out black clay, same size as the first wrap and finish making the eye cane, by wrapping it round the white layer.

The head will need 1/3 of whatever is left of the black clay. The rest will be for making the nose, the middle of the eyes and the ears. Make the head with the black clay. At this point, if you want a larger head for your cat, you can take some scrap clay (size of a cherry) and cover with the black clay. Make the head.
From the rest of the black clay make two tiny balls for the eyes, and one ball for the nose.

Make the ears from the laft black clay. Cut clay into two. Shape the ears as on the picture. Make two balls. Flatten each ball and point one end. The indent was made with a coctail stick.

Position the ears on the head. Make the white balls for the mouth. Make two equal size balls and one smaller. Assemble. Then add the small black ball for the nose. Put two holes on the side of the nose with a cocktail stick.

Now your cat can breathe! Make a small hole inside the mouth... it can yell at you... miaow.

What is left are the eyes. Cut two slices from the eye cane and position on the face. Your cat is blind no more.

Go on, make it a bow tie. You will have a very dapper cat. Bow tie is made from two tiny balls next to each other with a small one pressed between them. Indent with the cocktail stick to add character. Tilt slightly....even better. Place on the neck...The end.

The cool cat broken box

This is a distant cousin of Ginka puss. She is so cool. The bisque box had a lovely lid, which I managed to break before I left the shop, where I bought it. Clumsy me! Then I had an idea of damage limitation.

Looking at it now I am so pleased it worked. There are cats on each side of the box, all in different positions.

So the broken bisque box became a cute flower pot holder.

To stick the cats to the box I used the very sticky tacky glue. It is waterproof, and when dried becomes invisible. It is suitable for sticking polymer clay on card, pottery, wood, fabric and all painted surfaces.

When I have to stick polymer clay on metal, the best for me is the super glue gel. For sticking polymer clay on glass I use liquid clay, applying it before baking.

Morgan the Shih Tsu

His name is Morgan Evans, and I had the privilege to make him for a very nice man as a birthday present. Lots of people bought the Fimo needed and when I finished making him he was more that a stone heavy. I started quite small, but kept adding and changing and remaking him until I looked at Morgan, and knew he was ready.

With help Morgan went to be cooked. When I looked at his cute face in the oven I started shaking with laughter. "Am I done? Help, get me out of here!" he cried. I am sure he did not suffer - it was just a sauna.

Hamish

Dogs by Bonnie McGough

Hamish

The Westie

He is the first dog I ever made, and full of mistakes...but I still love him.

I have to tell you, this creature on the right is not a dog. In fact it is a cat!

While I was not looking, it came in and made himself at home so much that I did not have the heart to throw him out. That is why he has such a smug smile on his face.

Materials:
1 and 1/2 block light brown clay
1/2 block white clay
A little black clay
1/2 block scrap clay
Cooking foil

Betty - The dog

Are you a cat person or a dog person? Although I adore puppies and love dogs, I must confess I have never had a dog. But I hope there is time for me to have a dog one day.

Take the foil and make a small body, the same way as for the cat. Just make it a little shorter and a little fatter. We are making a cuddly little puppy.

Divide brown colours into six parts. Use two for front paws, two parts for back legs, one for the head and one for the ears and a small tail.

Cover the basic body frame with a thin layer of scrap clay. Condition white clay and roll out to place at the front of the body. Use most of the white clay, just leave small amount for the face of the dog. Take the clay allocated for the back legs. Divide into two and shape as on the picture. Place on the body pressing very gently.

Take the clay allocated for front paws and divide into two. Form the paws and place in the body starting from the bottom.

When you get to the neck, if the front paws are too long trim from the neck.

The clay for the ears and the tail divide into three parts. Use one part for each ear and the third part for the tail. Form and shape the ears and the tail as on the pictures.

Follow the pictures to form and shape the head, the front white patch of the face and the nose.

Just before you place the nose, indent a vertical mark on the white part of the face.

Here I go again sticking a cocktail stick in the dog's nose. I promise you no harm was done to any animal when they were made and later photographed. Honest!

Finish little Betty by making the eyes with black and white small balls of clay.

Betty is a dirty little puppy, so I shall get my wet wipes and wipe and clean her with lots of TLC.

She will be perfect in no time. Wooof!

And this on the left is Betty's new friend... Alfie.

Bonnie McGough
The frog...He is in love with
the doll.

Frog steps

Materials:
1 block light green clay
1/3 block light beige clay
1/8 block black clay
Red clay size of a broad bean
Tiny ball of white clay for eyes
1/2 block scrap clay

Take all green colour clay and condition.

Take all black clay and condition. Take from it a small ball for the eyes. The size of the ball should be about the size of a pea. Next, clean hands with wet wipes and take all beige colour. Condition well and make a slim cylinder. Leave aside.

Make a cane with the light green and the black. See instructions for simple cane. Flatten the green cane first by pressing with your hands and then with the roller. Position the slim beige cylinder as shown on the picture above and then roll the cane as shown. If the beige cane is longer, trim it. Roll the cane and allow it to overlap.

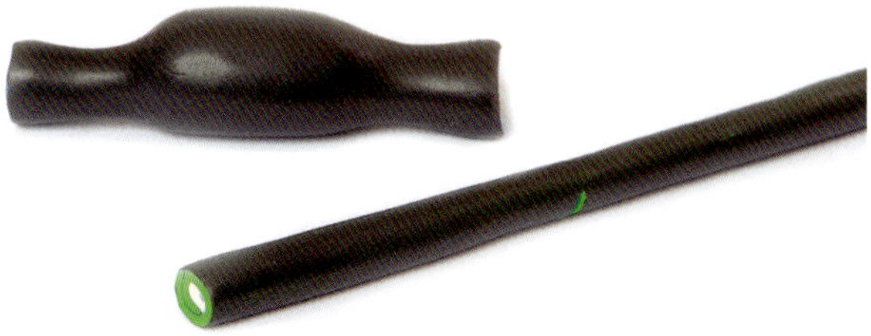

Reduce new cane by squeezing both ends and rolling the cane with the palms of your hands. Now you will have a very, very long rod.

Cut the rod into many shorter rods and stack together.

At this point I cut the stack across and position the two stacks next to each other.

Also, if you wish, you could remove the outer black by cutting it with a tissue blade. This is not normally necessary. Now you have the skin cane.

From the scrap clay allocate 1/3 for the body.

Divide the rest into two and use first half for the head and the rest for the back legs. Cut thin layers from the skin cane and cover the body shape. The back legs are kept straight until covered with a thin layer of skin cane. Then shape them as on the picture.

This is not a precise art, so you have a lot of flexibility in sizing and shaping the body, legs and front legs.

The front legs are made without any fill of scrap clay.

Cut two thicker layers of the skin cane and shape the front legs. At this point you can assemble the body with the front and back legs.

Flatten the ends of the limbs to create a more realistic look.

For this I used the wax carving dental tool. If you do not have the tool, use a cocktail stick. The legs do not have to be in the position shown, so if you want to change their position please do.

Use the last part of the scrap clay to cover the head with a thin layer of skin cane.

Make two balls with skin cane for the eyes. Flatten one end of each ball. The flattened end will be the base of the eye.

Take black clay and make two small balls for the eyes. Flatten them too. Make two white balls. Position white ball in the eye and finish with a small black ball for the centre of the eye.

Make the mouth and with a cocktail stick make a curved mark. If it is not even, it looks better. This is now your finished frog.

And here are some of the frog's friends.

Rex... The warrior rabbit

When my daughter was about five years old we had a little zoo, as you have when there are young children around and their mother loves all animals.

We had Laurence and Florence, the gold fish. Then Squeaky the black and white cat who wouldn't meaow.

But then came the Giant Rex.....a gargantuan rabbit with an even bigger ego. He was a handsome chap with his big fluffy ears and soft white bib.

I confess I don't remember his name, although it's possible I have blocked it out of my memory. He was my nemesis.

I cleaned his cage and dutifully fed and watered him. I saved him umpteen times from the allotment posse, who were after his scalp for gorging on their prize-winning vegetables.

Occasionally when in a good mood and not too full of himself, he would let me have a hug. But if I let my guard down, or he had a "bad day in the office" he would grunt and charge at me. At this point I would take to my heels and run as fast as I could, Olympic standard, to the back door and close the door firmly behind me. I can still see his angry eyes through the glass door.

The more I think about him now, the more I realise that he was a bad tempered terrorist.

He knew I was scared of him and he had the upper hand.

Well I may not remember his name, but I cared for this gorgeous bad tempered rabbit. So a few years down the line, after a few more sprints to the back door, the time finally came to make a decision on his fate.

We were moving to another town, house sold, bags packed, rabbit in his gigantic hutch. Then a friend popped in to say goodbye, and the conversation led to the fate of The Terrorist.

And that wonderful friend of mine professed to tell me how much she liked our gorgeous rabbit, and how much she knew about how to look after rabbits....

Well, with the greatest of pleasure I released him, hutch and all his toys to his new addoptive parent. And ran!

And he lived very happily ever after!

Materials:

1/2 block white clay
3/4 block light brown clay
Scrap clay for filling inside tummy and legs

Condition clay, starting with the white colour. With scrap clay form the shape of the white body and cover it with 2/3 of white clay Divide the light brown clay into 10 parts

Back legs two parts for each leg
Front paws two parts
Head 1 and 1/2 parts
Ears 1 and 1/2 parts
Paw pads and nose 1 part

Take four parts and use two for each of the back legs. Shape the back legs as pear drops. Make the front legs as shown on the picture from one part each.

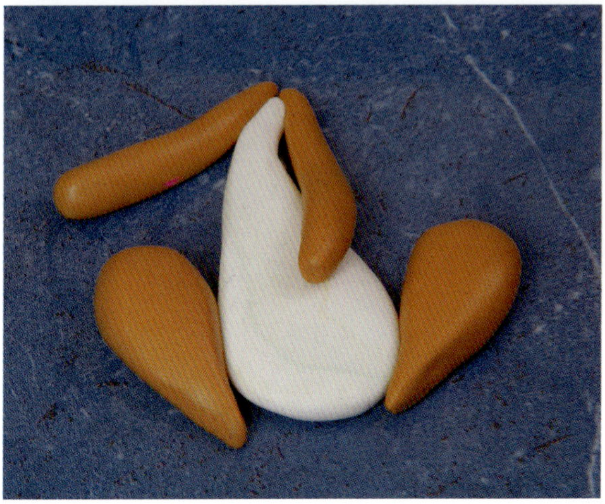

Add back paws to the body then position the front paws.

From the one part allocated for the paw pads take a small amount to make the nose, the size of a small 4mm ball.

From the rest of the clay make two pads. Make two larger balls and flatten for the larger white pads.
Then make eight white small balls for the paw pads. Size of the eight balls should be about 2mm. Place the white balls on the light brown balls, flattening them slightly.

First make the head in the shape shown.
Take a small amount of the white clay and make the mouth. Position mouth on the lower part of the head and finish by adding the nose.

Make two holes with a cocktail stick where the eyes are going to be and drop in each hole a tiny white ball. Finish the eyes by adding a miniscule black ball at the lower end of the eye.

Take the parts of light brown clay allocated for the ears. Divide in two. Make the ears in the shape shown on the picture.

You have less than a third of white clay left for the ears, but this is enough for the white parts. So make the white shapes for the ears and place inside the ears.

Flatten and point the ears. Position ears on head.
Make little dots on the mouth.

Your rabbit is ready!

Materials:

1/4 block white clay
1/3 block light brown clay
1/4 block dark brown clay
1/4 bronze clay
1/4 block black clay
Small ball of scrap clay

Condition clay and leave ready to use.

The top left pictures are a reminder of how to make a cane. For the front of the owl make a cane with half of the light brown clay. Flatten the cane with the acrylic roller.
The size to flatten the cane to is about twice the width of the cane.

Make a slim rod with half of the white clay and place on one side of the flattened cane.
Roll the cane allowing the cane to overlap.

Make the base of the body of the owl with scrap clay.

Cut thin slices from the cane and place, overlapping very slightly, on the front of the owl.

The young supervisor

Make a cylinder with the rest of the white clay. Wrap around it the quarter of light brown clay rolled out thick. Wrap it with a very thin layer of black clay.

Roll out the bronze colour and make a slim cylinder. Wrap around it a thick layer of light brown colour.

Flatten the first cane and place the bronze two colour cylinder on one side. Roll the cane and allow the outer cane to overlap. The colours can be changed very easily, this is only a guide of how to play with the canes. Cut slices from the cane and assemble the wings.

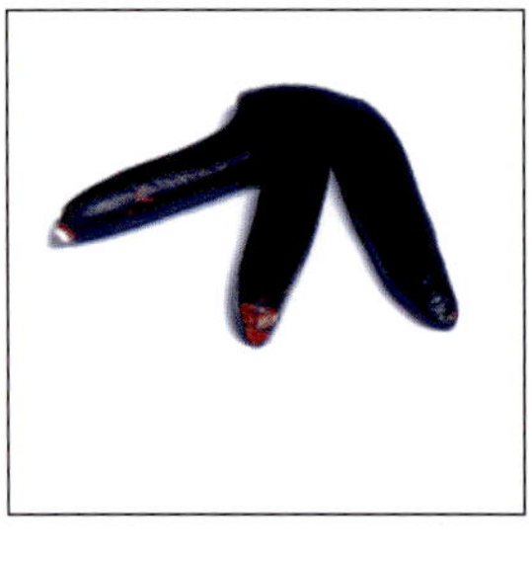

Make the ears from slices of the wing cane.
The legs with the claws are just three tiny black rods.

Materials for the eyes:
1/16 block white clay
1/16 block bronze clay
1/16 block black clay

The little helper

Make a white cylinder. Wrap with thick bronze. Then wrap with a thin layer of black clay. Reduce the cane and cut into four rods. Place rods side by side and squeeze to flatten. Make into a triangular shape cane. Cut into two and make a semi circle.

Cut into two again and make a circle. Reduce to the size you want the eye to be. Shape the ears from any of the canes you like.
They will look great. I chose the wing cane.
Make the legs from any black clay you have left.

The boss

The ladies

They are gathering to go to an all girls' night out.
Well...they certainly are dressed very well for the occasion.

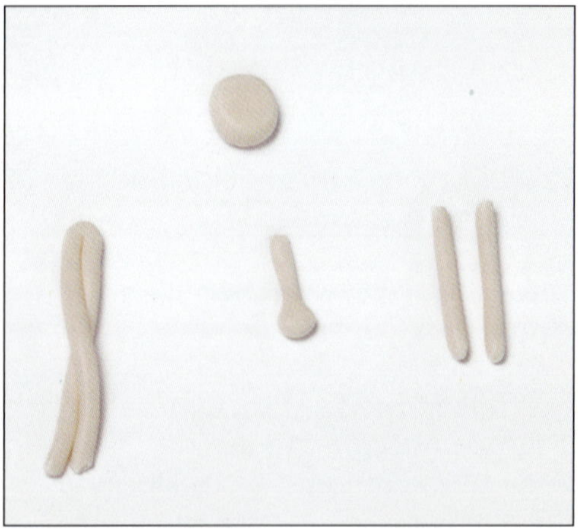

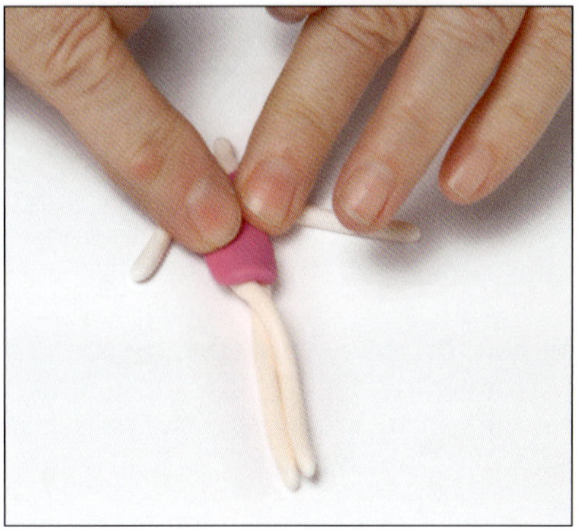

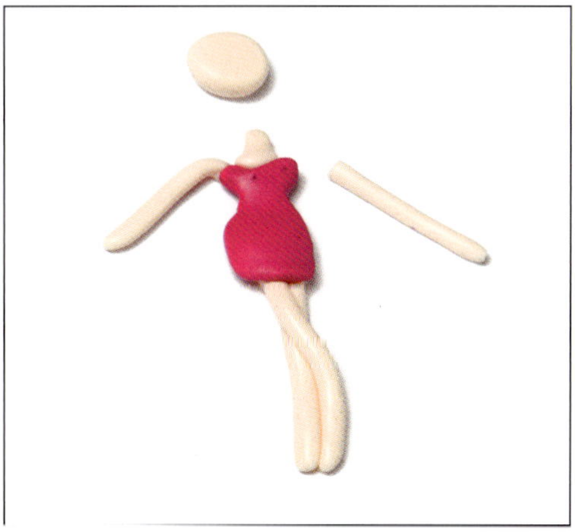

The lady

Materials:
1/3 block flesh colour clay
1/4 block pink clay
1/8 block brown clay
2 petite glass beads

Condition clay.
Divide flesh colour: use half of the clay for the legs.
For the head use a quarter of the clay.

Make a ball and flatten. From the remainder take a piece the size of a bean for the neck.

From the rest of the flesh colour you are going to make the arms.

First make the legs as two thin rods, twist to make them crossed.

Make the neck as shown on the picture.

Now make the arms the same way as the legs, but leave aside for placing on the body. Make a ball and taper on one end for the neck.

Take half of the pink and leave for the hat, shoes and lips.

With the rest of the pink clay make a thick rectangle. Pinch at both sides at a place above half of the rectangle. Make an indent at the top for the neck. Now assemble the figurine as shown on the picture.

The hair is made with the hair tool.

If you do not have an extruder or hair tool, then make the hair with very thin rods. Cut the rods to size, the length of the hair.

Place hair on the head - make an effort and give the lady a nice hairstyle.

Take a tiny ball for the lips and size of a pea for the shoes.

Make the hat with the rest of the pink.

The hat is made with two balls. Use a larger one for the brim - the main body of the hat and a smaller one for the top.

Flatten the larger ball and make an oval shape. Twist the oval to make the main body of the hat. Place it on the head. Then place the smaller ball on the top. As you are positioning it on the hat, press gently and flatten again slightly.

The hat is now ready too.

Now make two small balls and put at the end of the legs for the shoes.

Make a small hole on the face where the mouth is and drop a tiny pink ball for the lips. Touch the ball in the middle with the end of your tissue blade to make a line on the lips.

You can do this with a cocktail stick, but sometimes the end of a cocktail stick could be too thick.

Lastly, place the beads in the eyes' position.

Your lady is ready.

The Ballerina

Materials:
1/3 block flesh colour clay
1/3 block white clay
1/8 block brown clay
2 glass beads
A small amount of green clay

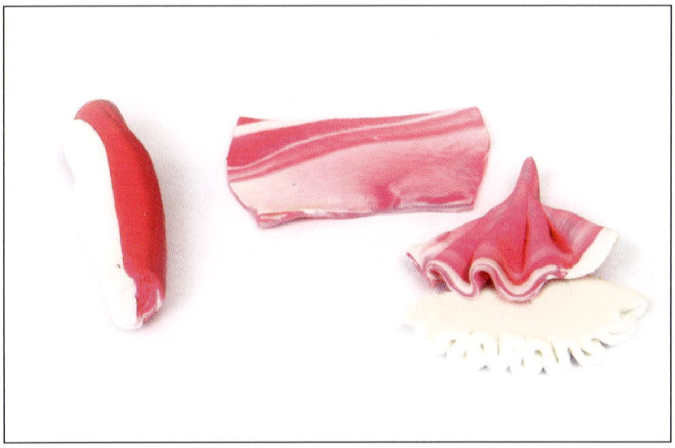

Condition clay. Take 1/3 of the white clay and make the frill. Roll out the white clay and make the frill by folding it like an accordion. Squeeze at the top to shape for the waist.

Take the pink clay and the rest of the white clay and mix the colours, by rolling the two colours together.

Follow by folding the two colours and then rolling again. Repeat the roll and fold until you are happy with the mixed colour.

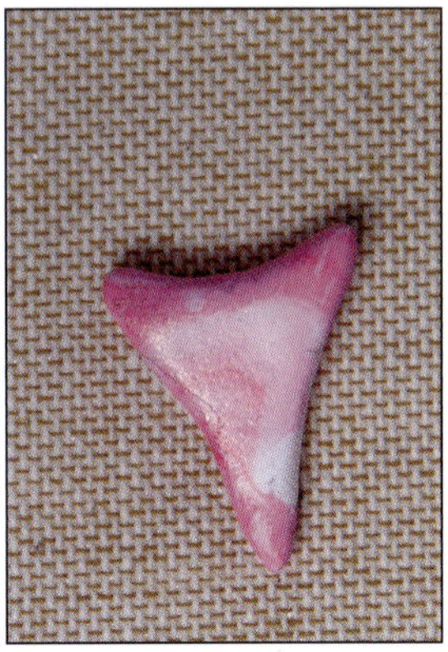

Take a small amount of the mixed colour to make the top of the dress and about six tiny balls for the headdress.

Also take one very tiny ball for the mouth and two small balls for the shoes.

From the rest, make the skirt the same way as the frill and position on top of the frill. Make the top as a triangle and indent the top for the neck.

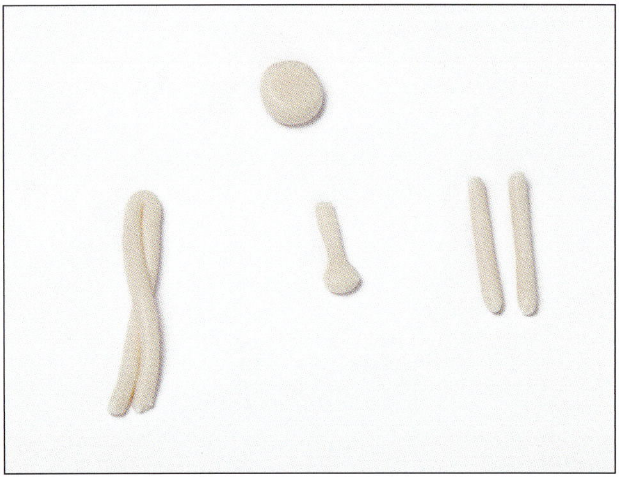

Join the bodice to the skirt and make sure you shape the waist line smoothly. The bodice should be standing with the sharp end just on top of the skirt.

Do not tuck it under.

Make the neck as shown on the picture. Make a ball and taper one end, add to the neck.

First make the legs as two thin rods, twist to make them crossed.

Now make the arms the same way but leave aside for placing on the body.

Make the head, by making a ball and flattening it slightly.

Assemble the body and arms and add the head to the neck.

The hair is made with the hair tool.

If you do not have an extruder or hair tool, then make the hair with very thin rods. Cut the rods to size, the length of the hair. Place hair on the head.

Make the headdress. Take the six tiny pink balls and make the same size green balls. Alternate to make the headdress and position on the head.

Position two beads for the eyes and one very tiny pink ball for the mouth. Shape mouth with the end of your tissue blade.

Bonnie McGough
Guardian Angel

The word 'angel' comes from the Greek word 'angelos' and means 'God's messenger'.

I do not know if you believe in angels, but I hope that if you are looking through the pages of my book they will bring you peace and love.

Thoughout my life I believe I had a beautiful angel standing at the bottom of my bed. As I could see him, for many years I thought that everybody could see their angel at night. Whether you can see yours or not, I believe that if you look hard enough you might just get a glimpse.

The first angel I made is busy taking care of the lady I gave it to at one of my demonstrations. She needed it more than me. I have made many angels since and most of them have flown away.

The following pages will show you how to make your own angels.

Materials:
3/4 block white clay
1/8 block flesh colour clay
1/8 block brown clay
Gold metallic powder
Tiny pink ball for lips
2 glass beads for eyes

Condition all clay, starting with the white clay. Divide the white clay, use 1/3 for the wings. Small pea sized ball for the halo.

Divide the rest into five parts. Take one part for the sleeves. Two parts for the frill and two parts for the main dress. The flesh colour is divided in three, 1/3 for the head, 1/3 for legs and 1/3 for the arms.

Separate the small piece of white clay for the halo, the size of a pea.

To make the wings take the white clay and condition it. Make a semi circle about 1 cm wide. With the flexible tissue blade cut the shapes to form the wings. Brush with gold powder.

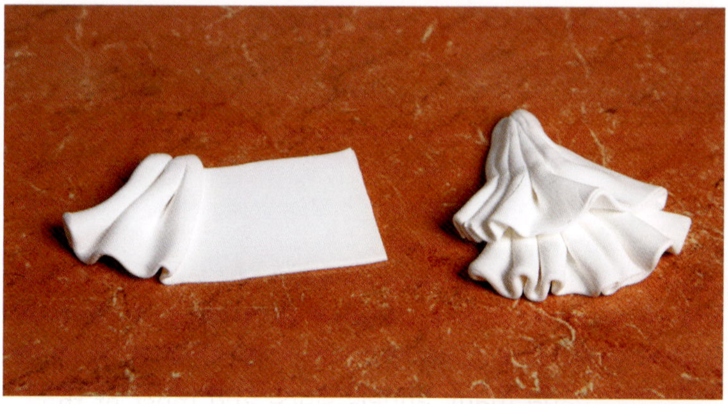

Take the white clay allocated for the dress and condition. Make the first frill, by rolling the clay thin and folding like an accordion. Make the top frill the same way. Squeeze the top to taper and elongate very slightly.

Condition the flesh clay and make the arms by making a small thin rod and cutting it in two.

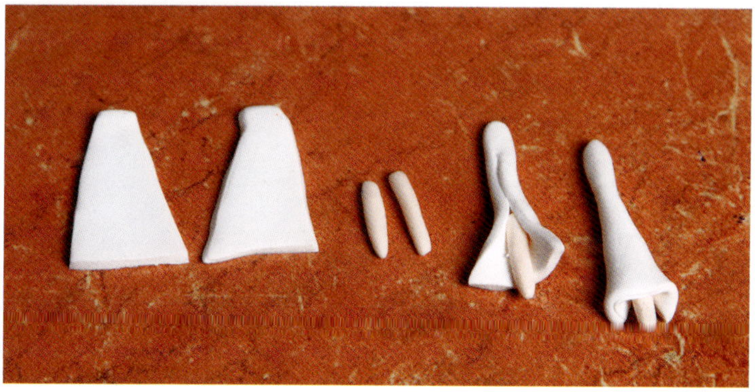

The sleeve are made by rolling out the allocated white clay into a rectangle and cutting into two. Place arm on the white rectangle and wrap the white sleeve around it. Taper the top end of the sleeve. Repeat for the second sleeve. Add the sleeves to the dress. Now you are ready to add the dress to the wings.

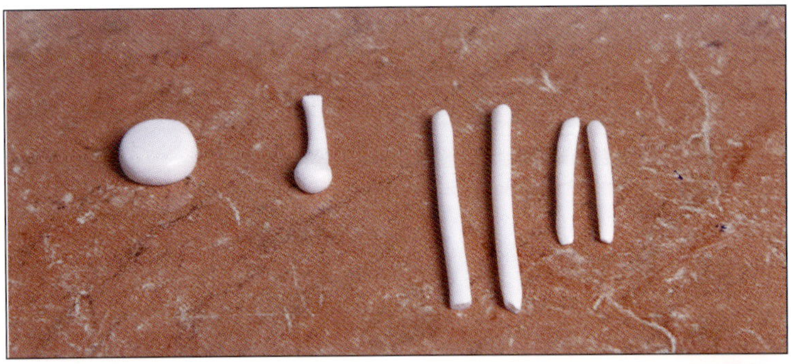

Make the face with flesh coloured clay. First make a ball, then flatten the ball and turn it upside down. The side that was on the tile will be nice and smooth, free of finger prints. This is the side you want for the face.

Make the legs the same way as the hands, just make them bigger. Position under the frill.

Next, position the body on the wings and add the head.

Make hair with the hair tool. Position hair on the head with the cocktail stick.

For the eyes and the mouth follow the same instructions as the lady on page 88

To make the halo, make a short 5 mm thick rod and form a circle. Place circle on top of the head.

Christmas angels

Kathleen Dustin
Seed Bead Neckpiece
The wonderful work of Kathleen Dustin

Bonnie McGough
Jewellery medley

The earliest beads found anywhere in the world are over 75,000 years old. The first beads were made with bone, shells, seeds and teeth and it is believed that they were originally made for religious purposes.They were worn for protection from evil and to bring luck. Later on beads were made with ostrich egg shell, bone, wood, glass and metals. Durring some periods in history the beads became used commercially and were a status in society.

Many of the old techniques and designs are still used today by contemporary artists and adapted for use with polymer clay. I have admired the excuisite beads made by Karen Lewis, otherwise known as Klew. I also love the innovative beads of Mike Buesseler and the very talented Kathleen Dustin. There are many fabulous books devoted to bead making with polymer clay and I can reccommend the books on beads and jewellery by Carol Blackburn and Linda Peterson for those wishing to develop their interest. Over the next few pages I will show you how to make a few simple beads to get you started.

Bead variations

One clay artist that has inspired me in the field of bead making is Mike Buesseler.

He has moved into different fields of art creations, but his influence and contribution in polymer clay bead making is remarkable. Here are some of my efforts in this field.

Materials:
Small amount of scrap clay
Any complex cane ends

With the scrap clay make a bead to your desired size. The bead can be in any shape - round, oval, square. Leave the beads so that they are ready for next stage.

Cut a slice out of the cane and roll out to about 3mm thickness. Then cut strips about 3mm wide. Twist strips by holding the two ends and twisting in opposite directions. Leave each twisted strip ready to use.

Take each scrap clay bead and starting from the top place the twisted strip on the bead.

When a strip finishes add the next strip starting from the end of the previous strip. The join will not show on the finished bead. Cover the whole bead, cutting any excess strip at the end.

The mobius bead

I love this bead. It took me some time to perfect. I was told it can't be made with old canes, but I beg to differ. At the beginning I found it quite difficult to manipulate the bead as first seen so I tried a different approach and now it is much easier.

But first a few words about the name of the bead. The bead is named after the continuous mobius strip invented in 1858 by a German mathematician and astronomer August Mobius.

As with many beadmaking techiques it was adapted for use with polymer clay.

One artist who has done some great work with mobius beads is Mike Buesseler.

For these beads I like to use complex canes. Sometimes I make very elaborate kaleidoscope canes, but very often I just throw some canes together: stack them together, wrap them with a contrast colour and sometimes cover with metallic gold powder. Here are some canes I made earlier!

Take whatever cane you are going to use and make the first decission: the size of your bead. The size of the bead will be determined by the size of your cane.
First, as your cane is circular at this stage, if it is too big reduce it.

Then change the shape from circular to square. Then slice the cane into two at 3 mm thick squares.

If you slice the cane too thick, when the bead is cured the end can separate.
Secondly, very gently warm the centre of the squire with your hands, moving your hands so gently that you do not mark the clay. By warming and softening the centre of your square, you will prevent the slice cracking at the edges when you start manipulating the square.

The idea is to bring the two opposite corners together, and the other two corners together but in the opposite direction.

With your index finger and thumb on the left hand start drawing the first two corners together, but not from the end of the corners.

Start from the centre.

Do the same with your right hand fingers, from the centre pulling very slowly and gently in the opposite direction.

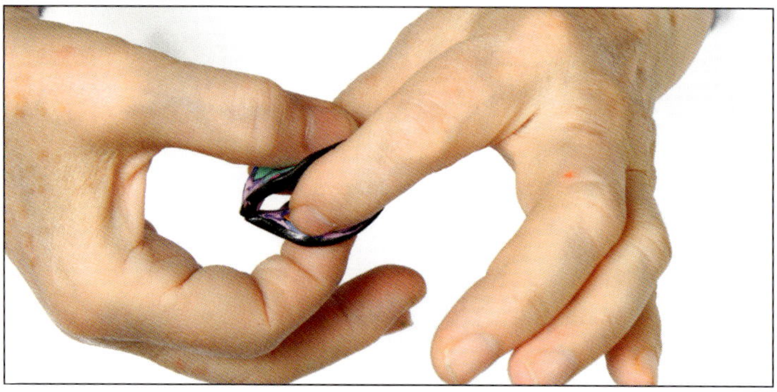

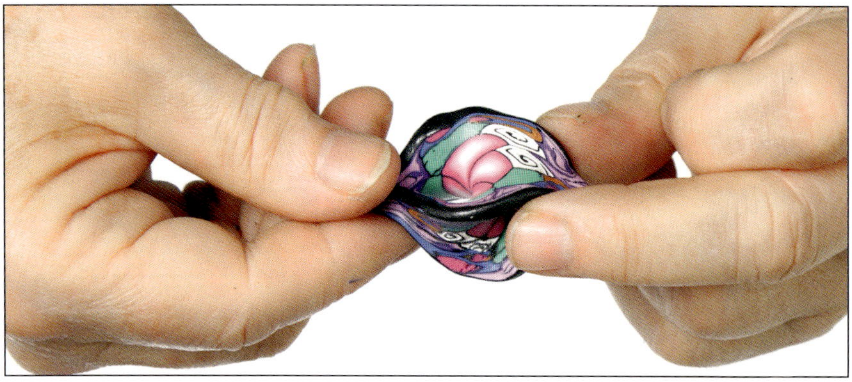

Please notice how the round shape of your fingers is slotting in the right places, shaping and manipulating the square and forming your mobius bead.

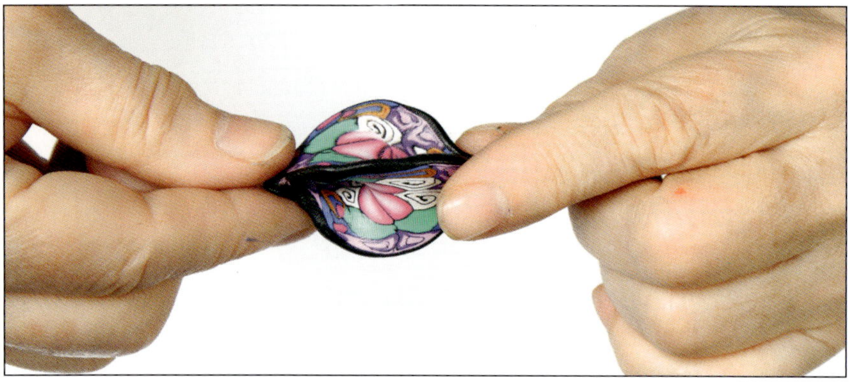

A few tips to know about this bead. Once the bead is formed, leave it to REST. Resting the bead helps in the bead staying together and makes piercing easier.

I would put the mobius bead with all the beads I have made on a plastic tray, and place in the fridge. The time in the fridge could be two hours to overnight.

Then I put a very fine glove on to touch the beads and pierce with my piercing tools, to make the hole in the bead.

Simple beads

I remember when we rolled out beads we made a long time ago with glue and colour pages from magazines. When we did not have glue, we improvised making the glue paste with flour and water. I don't remember how long the beads lasted, but making them was such fun

This page is about those old beads from bygone days. Use any canes, kaleidoscope canes, cane ends and any scrap clay you have available.

Make the cane into a triangle.

Place the cane on the tile and shape with your hands, by pressing the cane down on the tile. At the same time squeeze the top of the cane to form the pointed top end of the triangle. Keep pressing, squeezing and pulling apart gently.

It is not difficult to do. it just sounds a bit strange. But it works.

Do not pull apart too much, as it will make your triangle too small.

When you are satisfied with the size, apply gold metal powder to the cane.
The cane is now ready to be cut into the slices with which you will make the beads.

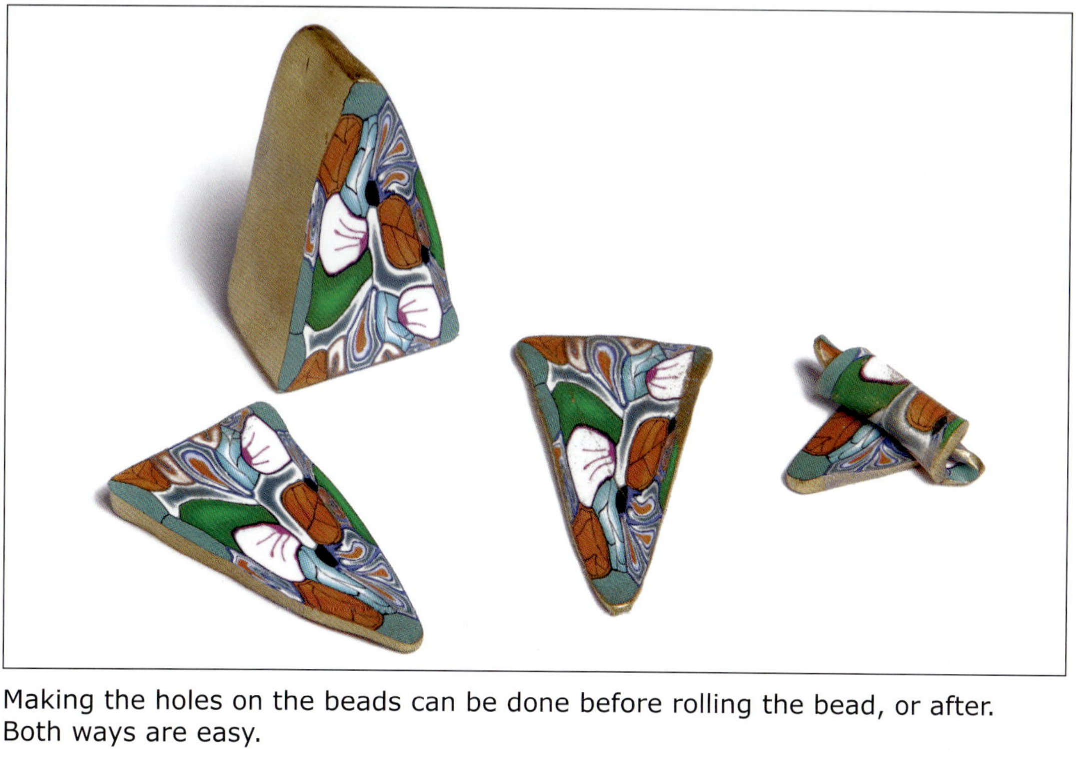

Making the holes on the beads can be done before rolling the bead, or after.
Both ways are easy.

Lentil bead

This bead I have seen many times made with glass squire, or acrylic plate.

For some reason I started making it by hand. For me this is much easier to do, but if you do not like this method, please feel free to use whatever works for you.

Whichever way you decide to do it the bead will be lovely.

For this bead I use scrap clay for the filler for the bead. On top, plain colours and the ends of canes and complex canes. It is one of the nicest beads to make and the results are so good. It does not take long to master, so have a try.

Important tip before making this bead: make sure your hands are very clean and dry.

Clean and dry your working surface very thoroughly.

As you are going to roll the bead between the palm of your hand and the working surface any dirty particles on both surfaces will transfer on to the bead.

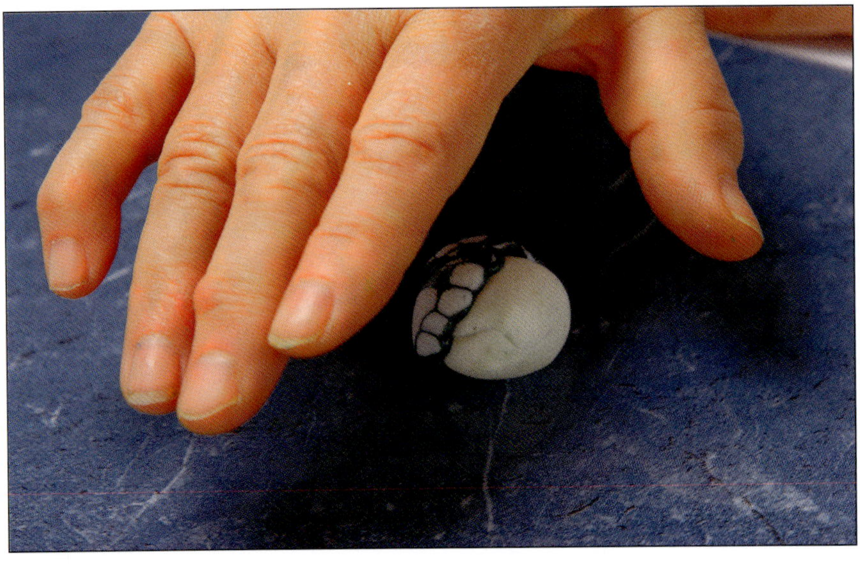

Place the bead on the clean working surface and, when using two contrast colours, or cane and plain colour, position it so it shows half and half the two different colour combinations.

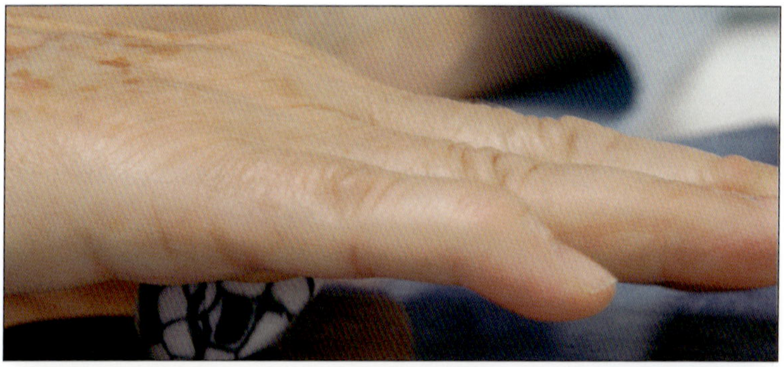

Place the palm of your hand on the bead. The bead should be in the middle of your palm. Apply only gentle pressure on the bead and start rotating the bead in a clockwise direction.

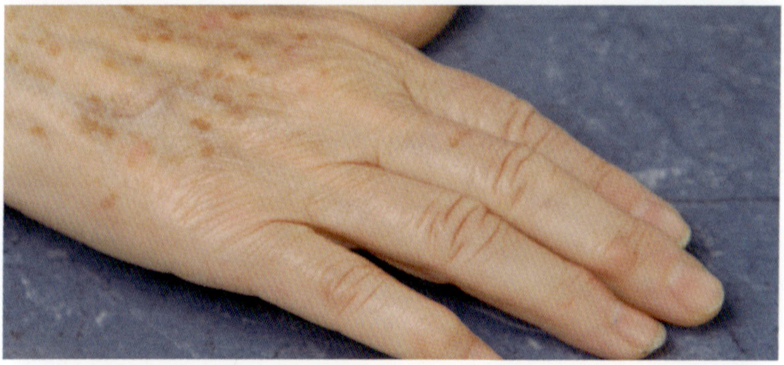

Keep rotating the bead, trying to stay in one place on the working surface.

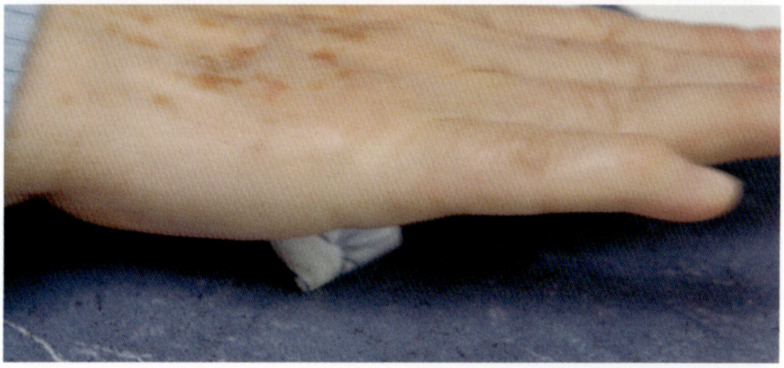

The bead, the hand and the working surface must be in constant touch, while you are rotating.

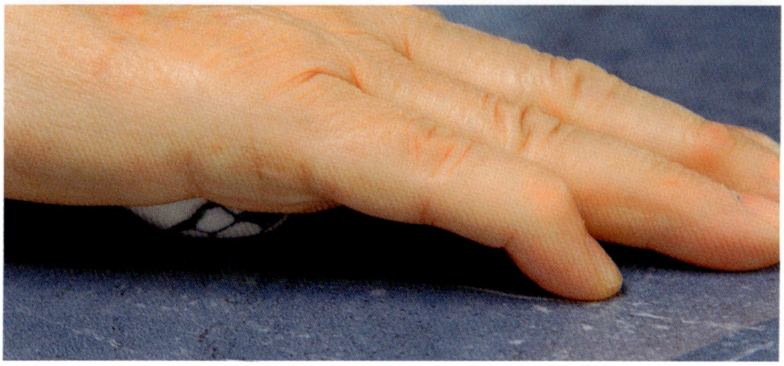

At any time you can lift your hand and check that the bead is starting to form a curl.

If the bead is not ready, place your hand on the bead and continue rotating.

The bead on the right may need a few more rotations.

Bonnie McGough
Lentil beads necklace

Bonnie McGough
Autumn colour necklace

Pendants

I can remember making my first pendant, having spent so many hours making the canes - then I spoiled it all. I started twisting the clay and messing with it and I was so surprised at the patterns on the clay.

The more I messed with the clay, the more I liked it.

So mess away, twist the clay, cut the clay, manipulate the clay... the results will always surprise and please you.

The picture on the left is a pendant I made while experimenting.

The best pendants I made were with the Mokume Gane and Millefiori techniques. Look for interesting blank pendant backings as this will help with shaping the pendant.Finally, do not be afraid to experiment.

The pendant on the right is from my bugs and lizards phase.

I found the pendant backing and I wanted to put something nice on it, but for a long time I could not make my mind up. The lizard just happen to stroll along on my tile and it was just right for the pendant. So he moved into his new home.

Here are some more pendants on different backings for you. When I make pendants with metal backing, I bake the pendant on the backing.

When the pendants are baked they come off the backing very easily. At this point wipe the back of the pendant and the metal part with alcohol or methylated spirit and then use superglue to attach.

Dry the two surfaces and add a few drops of good quality superglue.For me this method of gluing polymer clay to metal has worked very well.

There are lots of professional jewellery glues, but I have not used them. So far, I have glued Fimo to copper, Tibetan silver, brass, silver and the cheaper metals, and superglue has worked well.

Bonnie McGough
Millefiori on glass

Bonnie McGough
Bottles of hope

Bottles of hope

I love these little bottles. I don't know where they originated from, but when I came across them, I found their message of hope very appealing.

Even in our darkest moments of need, I believe that hope gives us the strength to go on. All the bottles on this page are filled with hope.

Naama Zamir
Vessels

Bonnie McGough
Egyptian cat

Gallery

Bonnie McGough

The zoo

Two young creatures from my own zoo

Gallery

Nina Stone

Beautiful pendants, beads and necklaces

Gallery

Loretta Lam
Come dancin’

Christine Dumont
Springtime

Gallery

Marie Segal
Stempunkgoddess

Bonnie McGough
Doll

Gallery

Marie Segal

Sue Heaser
Miniature silver clay jugs

Gallery

Maria Alexandrou

Gallery

Angela Smith

Penny Vingoe

Bonnie McGough
Kokeshi dolls

Bonnie McGough
Jewellery

Bonnie McGough

Aphrodite (Venus) Constantinou
Necklace

Bonnie McGough
Focal Beads

Acknowledgements

This book would not have been possible without the following people who have supported me along the way.

Rieka Hughes has been a source of gentle guidance throughout my work with polymer clay and I am extremely grateful for her support.

I would like to thank Russell Gibson, for his calm approach and valuable help in putting this book together.

My dear husband Philip who has supported me throughout.

Thank you Chris Prasetyo for all your help, not only with taking such wonderful images, but even for sorting out my computer when it decided to throw a wobbly and refuse to work.

Lots of thanks for Dr. Jude Therriot who, with his kind and creative help, finally got me started in writing the book.

With heartfelt thanks to my friend Terry Rawson, for being there for me.

For my Petchie, my little daughter Sophie a gigantic thank you for giving me help when I needed it most.

Many special thanks to the talented artists who so generously contributed to my book: Kathleen Dustin, Karen Lewis, Marie Segal, Sue Heaser, Jana Roberts Benzon, Naama Zamir, Christine Dumont, Loretta Lam, Barbara McGuire, Nina Stone, Maria Alexandrou, Aphrodite Konstantinou, Janice Cooper and Angela Smith.

A big thank you to STAEDTLER (UK) FIMO® for their support and encouragement.

And finally, deepest thanks to England, a country, which has given me a way of life which was denied to me in my early years and has enabled me to develop in my creative art and write this book.

About the author

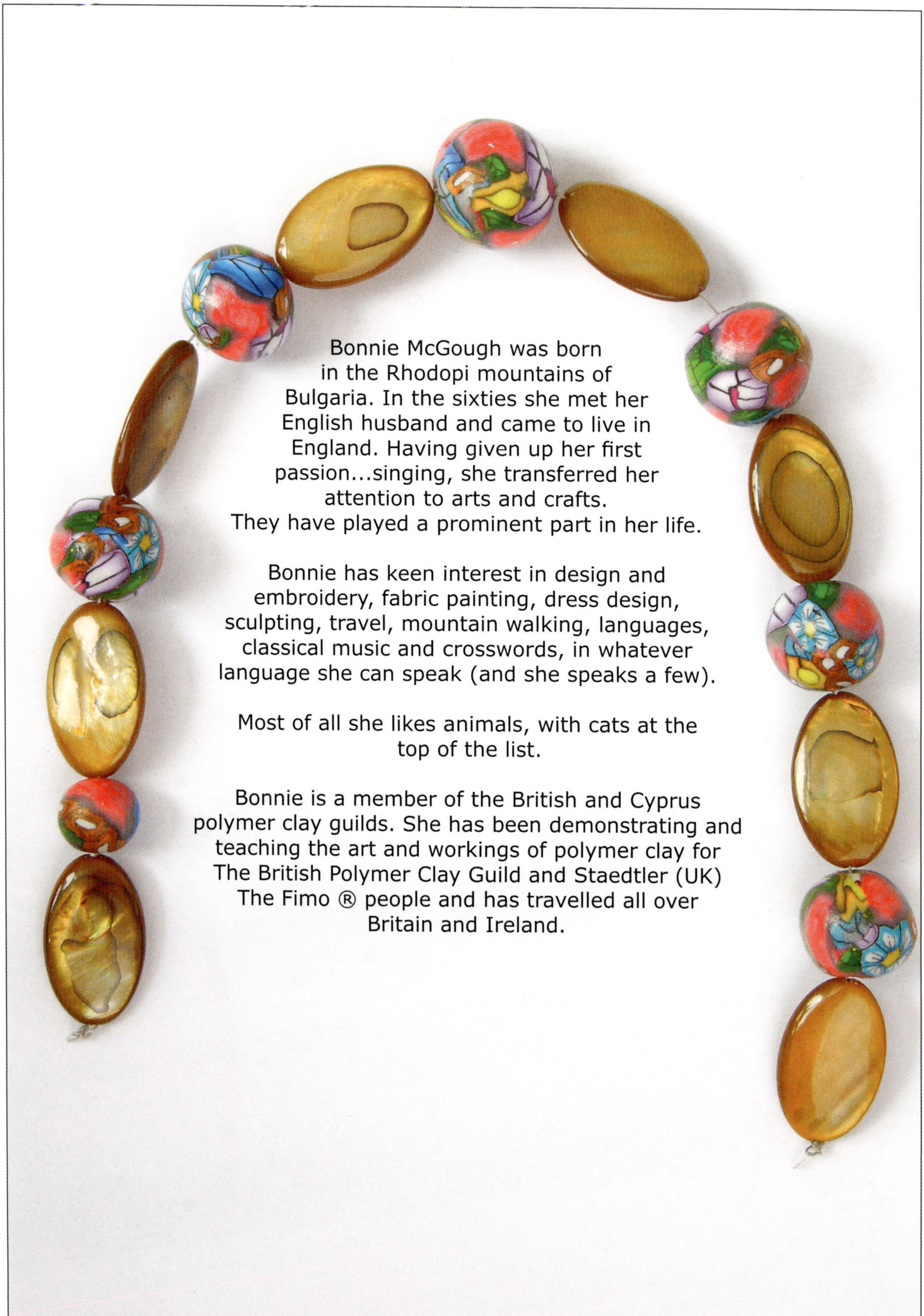

Bonnie McGough was born in the Rhodopi mountains of Bulgaria. In the sixties she met her English husband and came to live in England. Having given up her first passion...singing, she transferred her attention to arts and crafts. They have played a prominent part in her life.

Bonnie has keen interest in design and embroidery, fabric painting, dress design, sculpting, travel, mountain walking, languages, classical music and crosswords, in whatever language she can speak (and she speaks a few).

Most of all she likes animals, with cats at the top of the list.

Bonnie is a member of the British and Cyprus polymer clay guilds. She has been demonstrating and teaching the art and workings of polymer clay for The British Polymer Clay Guild and Staedtler (UK) The Fimo ® people and has travelled all over Britain and Ireland.